THE TOOLS OF MONEY

HANDS-ON FINANCIAL SKILLS
FOR TEENS, PARENTS, AND ADULTS

OBSTACLÉS
PRESS

ESSENTIALS SERIES

First Edition, March 2016
10 9 8 7 6 5 4 3 2 1

Published by:

Obstaclés Press
200 Commonwealth Court
Cary, NC 27511

lifeleadership.com

ISBN 978-0-9971212-3-0

Cover design and layout by Norm Williams, nwa-inc.com

Note: Some of the stories have had names, places and other details changed in order to maintain privacy or to more effectively illustrate the principles and ideas being taught.

Printed in the United States of America

"Ultimately, your money should work for you,
you should not work for it."
—Chris Brady

"Dollar bill: people spend their whole life seeking to earn
it, but won't spend 10 minutes seeking to learn it."
—Orrin Woodward

Contents

PART THREE: THINK LIKE THE BEST INVESTORS AND LEADERS

Money Is Important

Many successful people have learned and capitalized on a few basic truths that have made all the difference.
—U.S. NEWS AND WORLD REPORT

You are going to need some money in your life. You'll need it for food, living expenses, cars or other transportation, fun and entertainment, education and business, and many other goods. Money isn't the most important thing in life, but it does matter. Without it, many aspects of your life will be a major struggle.

Of course, this is obvious. What you might not realize if you are a teen is that most adults spend the large majority of their waking hours in life making a living, getting the funds needed to take care of themselves and their families.

This makes the topic of money even more important, for two big reasons:

- First, if you're going to spend a huge part of your life working, you might as well make good choices about what kind of work you'll be doing. If you do something you love, something that really makes a difference in the world, and something you care about, you are going to enjoy a lot more of your life than people who get stuck in jobs they don't much like. The truth is, about 20 percent of people really like their work—and 80 percent don't. You want to be part of the 20 percent, right?

- Second, with all that time spent working during your life, it's important to make enough money that you can actually pay your bills and also live the kind of life you really want. For example, if you have to work 80-hour weeks your whole life, you won't have much left for family. If that's important to you, make good choices about your business and career and what kind of work you choose for your life.

Young people have a lot of options in choosing how to make a living, so think about this early on, and choose wisely. And if you're older, you can still make powerful decisions that will determine how you spend your days, work time, and life. If you are going in the wrong direction, consider how to turn things around. Don't wait. Make the decision right now that you're going to choose and live the life you actually want.

The younger you are, the easier this choice is for most people. Either way, this book is going to show you how to earn the money you need, take care of it effectively, and live the kind of life you really want to experience and enjoy.

The focus of this book is on specific, essential tools of money and finances and how to use them well. But always remember that the true purpose of these tools is to help you live your best life. That's why these tools are so important, because if you learn to utilize them effectively, you'll have the resources and opportunities you really want.

As best-selling author and business leader Chris Brady put it: "Twenty years from now, what will you wish you had done today?"

This is a very important question. In twenty years, your life will be different. But whether it is better or worse, and whether you'll be living the life you truly want, is up to you. In fact, the decisions you make now will hugely influence where you are and what you'll be doing in twenty years.

Moreover, the financial decisions you'll make right now and in the coming weeks (as you learn and apply the tools in this book) are going to drastically impact where you end up in your life. If you read this book and implement the tools it outlines, you'll be at a much better place than if you don't.

> **Always remember that the true purpose of these tools is to help you live your best life.**

Not everyone learns the tools of successful leadership, money, and finances. In fact, most people don't.

We invite you to be one of the few who do this differently. Learn about financial fitness and the tools of money right now—and apply them. If you are a teen, this will set a tone for your entire life. And if you're older, now is the time to make this happen.

In just twenty days, applying the tools in this book can make a major difference in your life. In twenty months, you'll be on a much better path toward the life you truly want to live. And in twenty years, if you keep applying these financial tools, you'll be living your life in ways you might not even dream about right now—and you'll almost certainly be helping other people do the same.

This is exciting! This is not just another book you hold in your hands. These tools are powerful, and they work. They work if you're a teenager, and they work if you're the teenager's parent. They work for anyone. But you have to understand them, and you have to apply them.

If you do, you'll be far ahead of many others who, for whatever reason, don't know these tools or simply aren't using them. And you'll build your best life.

One more thing. It's never too early to learn and get started on this. If you're only nine years old, or 13, excellent! Start learning and applying the tools of money and leadership right now. If you're 15, or 17, or 24, or any other age, from 25 to 95, these tools work. They'll increase your power, and they'll boost your effectiveness.

If you use them.

YOUTH
Call to Action

A. What do you want to be doing twenty years from now? Really? Think about it and write down your answers. Brainstorm options.

B. What don't you want to be doing twenty years from now? Write these answers down as well.

C. Discuss your answers to A and B with your parents.

PARENTS AND OTHER ADULTS
Call to Action

1. Complete Exercises A and B above, for yourself. Write your answers.

2. What are you going to need to change in your life in order to ensure that you get what you want (and don't get what you don't want) in the next ten years? Write these down as well. Then do the same with twenty years.

3. If it won't cause an argument, discuss these findings with your spouse. If it will cause an argument, you probably need this book even more than most people do. If possible, make a plan with your spouse to read each chapter together and gently—kindly, in positive, uplifting tones—talk together about what you are learning.

"Actions speak louder than words...."

PART ONE

A SOLID FOUNDATION
FOR SMART MONEY

"From little acorns mighty oaks do grow...."

TOOL #1

Youth Allowances that Build Leaders

Fifty Billionaires Were Asked: "To what do you most attribute your success?" They answered: "Discipline and Hard Work (35), Willingness to Take Risks (24), Education (10), Intelligence (10), Inheritance (3)."
—GEORGE BERNARD SHAW

On the One Hand

It's very important for young people to learn to manage their money and gain good habits of financial fitness. This doesn't happen very often unless Johnny or Tami has some money and gets to make financial choices. And the best results occur when they get money periodically and have to manage it consistently over time.

Imagine if Tami's money management experience is limited to "Mom, my shoe has a hole in it. Can you buy me a new pair?" She's not going to learn how to follow good financial principles.

At some point, young people need to have real, hands-on

> It's very important for young people to learn to manage their money and gain good habits of financial fitness.

15

experience with money. And it is much better if this occurs long before they leave home.

Yes, each youth needs to be taught the basic principles of financial fitness—but he also needs to *practice* them as well. To use them. To learn by doing. This occurs much more effectively—and the results are far better—under the direct guidance of an attentive parent.

Because of this, an allowance can be very helpful in raising children who understand money and financial fitness. By receiving regular income, Tami learns to save, spend, and give correctly, according to sound principles. This is an important (nay, *vital!*) part of learning for every young person.

On the Other Hand

With that said, what financial principles does a young person learn when she is handed money every week, no matter what she does or doesn't do, and with no strings attached? There are adults who live this way, but nobody can say that this is a positive method of teaching or living sound financial principles.

If the kids become accustomed to money just coming in regularly without being earned, they're learning the wrong lessons. For this reason, many parents resist giving allowances to their children. At first, this makes sense. But there is actually a better way.

> **Each youth needs to be taught the basic principles of financial fitness—but he also needs to *practice* them as well.**

Solution: The Brady System

Here is the system used by Chris and Terri Brady with their children, and it is very effective. In fact, it is used by many other families as well and nearly always with very good results.

First (and this is very important), there are certain duties and responsibilities given to each child and youth in the family that are just expected because the young person is part of the home. Each child learns that he must do his share and not expect to be paid for it. No allowance for these chores.

Second, as a child grows and becomes capable of additional responsibilities, she can "earn" an allowance by fulfilling special duties. Have a standard list of chores that a child must continually perform in order to earn her allowance. This way the allowance isn't a welfare payment, but the young people do have the opportunity to get money regularly and learn how to manage it effectively.

Third, parents carefully teach each child about saving, giving, and spending—the guidelines, pitfalls, and wise choices. In fact, parents teach each child all the tools outlined in this book, each at the right time in view of the child's maturity. In the case of allowance money, the very basic tools of saving, giving, and spending are the key. (More on these later.)

There is an old saying that in successful families there are only a few rules, but they are lovingly and firmly enforced. Unsuccessful families might have lots of rules or no rules, or they might be angrily, haphazardly, or loosely enforced. But when you find a successful model of raising kids, it's worth learning about.

Likewise, families that successfully teach their children to be financially fit find a way—like the Brady System outlined here—to get the children and youth periodic money to manage, ensure that they actually do something worthwhile to earn it, and then closely and personally help them learn and apply the principles of what to do with their money.

Those who follow this pattern nearly always raise youth and young adults who know how to effectively manage their finances. This is an incredibly valuable skill to learn and, if you are a parent, to teach your children.

It is also the starting point of financial fitness, the foundation of everything that comes later. Teach a child how to successfully apply the basics (earn your money, save, give, spend wisely), and he's firmly on a path to sound financial fitness. But he needs to practice it, and the sooner the better.

> **Parents carefully teach each child about saving, giving, and spending— the guidelines, pitfalls, and wise choices.**

Different Strokes

Of course, every family is different, and parents often like to do things their own way. That's how it should be. But this should not be an excuse for ignoring the valuable lessons of financial fitness. When it comes to finances, a failure to learn the principles of good finances on the one hand, and of earning your way on the other hand, is frequently a serious problem. It may not seem like a big deal right now, but when the young person moves on to adulthood, poor financial habits frequently become a huge source of pain which can last for decades, or even more.

Many families who want to teach finances without an allowance end up with adult children who struggle mightily to get their finances in order. Some never do. On the other extreme, many families who want allowances to be "free from chores" end up with young adults who chronically overspend—and keep returning to Dad and Mom for financial help long after they have moved on to adulthood.

The families who follow the simple but effective pattern outlined here tend to see much better results. To repeat:

- Everyone has family and household chores, and nobody gets paid for them.
- The kids who are capable of additional responsibilities and specially assigned chores can do them and "earn" an allowance.
- Parents help each child learn to plan, budget, save, give, and (sometimes) spend each time he or she receives the allowance.

Learning these basic lessons, along with the other tools covered in this book, is a powerful foundation for youth and young adults to wisely manage their money. Without the basics, the more advanced lessons often fail to sprout or flourish.

Adults can also learn a lot by studying this system. Even if you aren't a parent, just knowing how this works will help you get a clearer view of effective money management.

> **When it comes to finances, a failure to learn the principles of good finances on the one hand, and of earning your way on the other hand, is frequently a serious problem.**

Guidelines

Since this is so important, let's go a bit deeper. Allowances should nearly always be based on additional chores, individual responsibilities that each child or youth does to "earn" his or her allowance. If the child is too young to understand this, or to follow through, he really doesn't need an allowance anyway, and at this stage he's not going to learn much about managing money.

When a child is ready to take on more responsibility, and live up to it, she is given basic chores in the family. Everyone has them, and nobody gets paid to do them. When the child is ready to take responsibility for even more special duties, she begins to earn an allowance that is attached to satisfactory fulfillment of these assignments.

It is important to explain this clearly to each child. In fact, in most families the parents and later the older siblings end up explaining it a number of times.

Food, Clothes, Electronics, and Other Stuff

As the young person grows up, this all gets much more serious. One thing every parent can count on: At some point almost every youth is going to want some things beyond a roof over his head, food at the family dinner table, and whatever clothes and other "stuff" Mom and Dad decide to give him. He might crave special activities, certain clothes that he thinks are cool, cutting-edge electronics, and a host of other things.

When this happens, a whole world opens up to the youngster. He sees that some people have more, and others have less. He realizes that his choices in life will very likely impact what he has later on as an adult.

But what the young person might not quite realize yet is that such choices are already happening, even though he is very young. If he learns the wrong lessons, or simply doesn't learn the right financial lessons, he won't know how to be financially fit. Of course, that's not the goal most parents have for their children, but it happens a lot anyway—to the majority of people, in fact.

And this problem (not knowing the principles of financial fitness) will be a drag on his life until he learns and applies them.

Choose Your Option

For example, consider the following two dialogues between a father and a son:

Option 1: Tom (age 24)

"Dad, I can't make the payment on my car this month. Can you send me $850?"

"Wow. Tom, that's how much I sent you last month, and the month before that. When are you going to be able to make your car payment on your own?"

"I'm not sure, Dad. Things have been pretty tight. Can you send it tonight?"

"Actually, I've been meaning to talk to you about this. Do you really need a car with such high payments? I mean, $850 is a lot more than many families pay for their housing every month. Maybe you need to downsize. I can't keep sending you money all the time like this."

You can already guess where this conversation is heading. Tom probably thinks his dad is being a jerk, and Dad knows

Tom needs a big attitude adjustment. Maybe Dad will just keep sending the money—it seems like he's been doing that for years. Or maybe he'll refuse and Tom will be left to his own devices. Or maybe Tom is in real trouble somehow. It certainly appears that Tom is wasting money and that his dad is an easy target.

Either way, Tom doesn't understand financial fitness. And he needs a big dose of it—fast. But it doesn't seem very likely that he'll get it anytime soon, does it? His dad should have been teaching sound finances many years ago. Of course, we don't know everything about Tom from this short dialogue. He may be doing some things well in his life that we can't see from the dialogue, but ownership, initiative, ingenuity, and PDCA (Plan Do Check Adjust), among others, don't seem to be among them.

And people who are financially fit will clearly see that Tom and his parents didn't follow the allowance system outlined in this chapter. Tom simply doesn't exhibit any of the traits or ways of doing things that the Brady System teaches a young person. Tom is missing the basics.

However this situation turns out, it is likely to be bad. Either it will cause more (and probably even bigger) problems for both Tom and his dad, or it will bring a major conflict to a head right now. Tom needs to understand the tools in this book.

Option 2: Eric (age 12)

"Dad, I really want a mobile phone," Eric said.

His dad looked at him and smiled. "How much does a mobile phone cost, and how much are the monthly fees for it?"

"Uh...." Eric wasn't sure.

"Well, what are you going to do about it, and how can I help?"

Eric agreed to research the costs of a mobile phone and the monthly bill.

The next day he told his dad, "You were sure right. I didn't even bother looking up the price of a mobile phone, because when I researched how much it costs per month, I couldn't believe it. I don't need to spend $60 or more a month for a phone connection. Why would I? All my friends have phones, and I can just borrow theirs if I ever need one."

His father smiled again. "I thought you might come to that conclusion. I looked into it as well, and we can add you to our account for a little less—around $40 a month. It's up to you. I think you're wise to really consider the pros and cons on this."

Eric thought about that for a few seconds, then he shook his head. "I just don't need it that much. My friends text, play games, and use a bunch of different apps on their phones. But if I'm paying for it, it's just not worth that much to me."

His dad rubbed his chin and replied, "I know parents in some places pay for their kids' phones because it's a safety issue. And that's why sometimes we have you take my phone or Mom's with you to certain events. That totally makes sense to me. But here it's not important to your safety for you to have your own phone, so we feel that if you want one, you should pay for it. And there would be some other rules on how you can use it, just like when you use the Internet."

"I agree," Eric responded. "I like paying my own way as much as possible. It's like you always say, I need to learn how to use money before it's a matter of real survival. When I go away to college or start my next business, I want to be good at managing my finances."

> **I need to learn how to use money before it's a matter of real survival.**

In contrast to Tom, Eric is strong on some basic financial instincts. He may not know exactly what his life purpose is yet (after all, he's only 12), but he knows enough about it to say: "When I go away to college or start my next business, I want to be good at managing my finances."

One gets the feeling from reading Eric's words that if he really saw the value of paying for a phone, he'd quickly muster the creativity and ingenuity to earn the extra money. But he's looked it over, weighed his options, and he's just not ready to pay $40 or $60 a month for something he doesn't value more highly. If he ever does value it that much, it's clear that he'll just earn the extra money and afford it without giving it a worry.

These two scenarios (Tom and Eric), which are extreme on purpose, could hardly be more divergent. The attitudes of the dads and the sons are drastically different. In Option 1, nobody seems to clearly understand financial fitness, while both participants in Option 2 have a good grasp of sound money management.

But there's more. In truth, the conversations between Eric and his father are like many found in homes and relationships where the allowance guidelines suggested above are followed. Note how Eric understands the concepts of personal responsibility, forgoing something now in order to really earn it, and paying his own way. He gets it. He is learning financial fitness—and living it.

Tom is more than a decade older than Eric, but in terms of finances, Eric is much more mature. In fact, read closely, and it becomes clear that Tom's lack of maturity isn't just limited to finances. The way Eric learned about financial fitness has helped him act and choose maturely in many other ways as well.

Also note that as long as Eric's father keeps treating him (and teaching him) the way he has so far, Eric is probably never going to end up like Tom. Not at age 24, not ever. And as long as Tom's dad keeps treating and teaching Tom the way he does, they're both in trouble.

Which Scenario Do You Want?

If you are a teen reading this book, do you want to be like Eric or like Tom? And who do you think your parents want you to be like at age 24?

Even more important, if you are like Tom when you are 24, do you

> Note to parents: the power of the right kind of allowance system is huge—the young person learns all the right lessons, none of the wrong ones.

think you'll be on track to live your best life and truly achieve your biggest dreams and life purpose? Or even to have happy relationships and make ends meet when each month's bills come along? Clearly not. Tom can change, of course, but it's much better to get on the right track in the first place.

Eric understands money at a level Tom hasn't even dreamed of. (Note to parents: the power of the right kind of allowance system is huge—the young person learns all the right lessons, none of the wrong ones.)

If your parents don't use the Brady System, or something a lot like it, you can still learn the right lessons by applying the tools in this book. But if they do, thank them for teaching you this incredibly valuable lesson. People who know how to manage money well are way ahead of those who don't.

One More Review

The right kind of allowance is a very powerful and effective way to teach young people how to be financially fit. Do you remember all the details of how to do this? There are only three, but each is very important. We've repeated them several times already, but it's worth another go. Once more:

1. Each child and youth in the home has family and household chores, and nobody gets paid for doing them.
2. The kids who are capable of additional responsibilities and chores can do them and earn an allowance.
3. Parents help each child learn to plan, budget, save, give, and—sometimes—spend when he receives his allowance.

To Parents: We'll have more to say about number 3 in later chapters. But knowing and using these three simple principles is an incredibly effective way to teach financial fitness to your children.

> **People who know how to manage money well are way ahead of those who don't.**

To Youth: If you are being trained this way, be grateful. Do your best to learn these important lessons and always follow them. If, on the other hand, you don't have the opportunity to learn the lessons of financial fitness this way, take good notes and use this book to learn what you'll need. It will take a little more work, but you can do it.

YOUTH
Call to Action

A. Work with your parents to set up a good allowance system in your home. Make sure they've read this chapter so they understand what you're asking of them—and that you're not just seeking free money.

B. If this option isn't available to you, keep track of any money you earn or receive for any reason, and follow the principles outlined in later chapters.

PARENTS AND OTHER ADULTS
Call to Action

1. Study the guidelines in this chapter, and set up an effective allowance system in your home.

2. Meet with your kids, announce the plan, and follow through. It can be very helpful to write out the three simple principles of the plan and post it somewhere visible in the home. Make this announcement and the follow-through positive and fun, so it never feels like an imperial decree.

3. Each time you pay allowances, help each child make good financial decisions (specifics will be covered in the following chapters).

"Experience is the best teacher...."

Be Professional

People decide in October that they're going to change their behavior in January. That doesn't work. If they were truly resolved, they'd start that night.
—ORRIN WOODWARD

Every Time

Children, teens, parents, and all adults: Whenever you get any money—earned, gifted, or anything else (including an allowance)—do something very important with it. In fact, do this immediately when you get paid. Divide it into three piles: Save, Give, and Spend.

But don't divide it into equal piles. Not at all.

Here's why. If you want to be successful at anything in life, there is an incredibly effective way to do it. First, find people who have already done it, who are already successful at it. Second, learn from them, and emulate how they did it.

> If you want to be successful at anything in life, there is an incredibly effective way to do it. First, find people who have already done it, who are already successful at it. Second, learn from them, and emulate how they did it.

In terms of finances, this means the following: Don't take money advice from people who are broke! Think about it. Anything they tell you is likely false, or at the very least, they don't understand it enough to do it themselves. So you would be very unwise to take their advice.

Take the advice of people who have done it—who have money, who are making money, and who are doing it with integrity and wisdom. Follow leaders who are actually good leaders, and learn about money from those who are truly financially fit.

With that in mind, here's how this book came about. Two very successful business leaders, Chris Brady and Orrin Woodward, outlined the principles of financial success and good money management in an excellent best-selling book entitled *Financial Fitness*. Later they outlined the principles of financial success for youth in another best-selling book: *Financial Fitness for Teens*.

> **Whenever you make or receive any money, the first thing you should do is save some of it. Saving is your first step, every time.**

The book you are reading right now is a third book built on their teachings about the principles of financial fitness. This one focuses on the tools, the how-to, the hands-on specifics of true financial fitness. This book teaches you exactly *how* to do what is needed.

In the first two books, and now in this book as well, Brady and Woodward recommend the same thing about money:

Always Save.
Always Give.

Spend Wisely.

Build Assets.

Let's begin by focusing on the first two of these important guidelines to financial fitness, then we'll address the others in later chapters.

Always Save

Whenever you make or receive any money, the first thing you should do is save some of it. Saving is your first step, every time you earn or receive money.

If you don't save any of the money you've obtained, you don't get to keep any of your money.

Think about that for a second. If you get money and then spend it all, what part of the money do you get to keep? None. It's all spent. If you get money and then give it all away, which part is yours? Answer: you don't have a part. It's all been given to someone else.

One great classic book, *The Richest Man in Babylon*, teaches that all financially fit people always do the same thing: They put a preplanned percentage of all money that comes to them into their savings. This pile is essential.

We'll discuss actual types of savings—from the piggy bank to a savings account—in a later chapter. But right now it's essential to learn this one lesson. People who don't save are not financially fit, and they'll never get ahead.

This may seem blunt or super obvious, but it is true. Only people who save will ever get ahead financially. And "saving" doesn't mean that once in a while you haphazardly stick a few bills in the bank. "Saving" means that every time you get money, you save a predetermined percentage of it.

Period.

Always.

People who do this become financially fit. Almost all of them are able to fully live their great life purpose.

People who don't do this are nearly always broke. They struggle to make ends meet, and they struggle to live their life purpose. They usually just don't have the funds to get by.

Every time you get money, save a predetermined percentage of it. And keep it saved.

But How Much?

So how much should you save each time you get money? What is the best predetermined percentage to put into savings?

The truth is, this differs, depending on the person and his or her situation in life. But here are a few key guidelines:

- In the book *Financial Fitness*, Chris Brady and Orrin Woodward teach adults to always put 10% of any income to tithing and another 10% to long-term savings. This means you put it there and don't spend it. You can move it into another kind of savings (which we'll explain in later chapters), but it's always your savings. And it grows every time you get any money.

  Also, in addition to this 20 percent, give a little more to other good causes.

- Brady and Woodward also teach adults to take some money every time they get any and build up at least $1,000 of extra cash in an emergency fund. This helps when the dryer breaks, the car needs repairs, etc. Keep building this fund until you have at least $5,000 stashed away for emergencies.

Note that all this comes *before* you spend your money: 10% tithing, 10% savings, a little to charity, and a little to your emergency fund (until you get it up to $5,000).

- *Financial Fitness for Teens* teaches that teens nearly always have fewer expenses than adults and should put away a higher percentage than most adults can manage. Like adults, teens should have a predetermined percentage for tithing, other giving, and saving. The savings percentage should be discussed and worked out between the teen and her parents. And once it is decided, she should always stick to it and follow through.

  If they choose to alter the percentages later, fine. But whatever percentages are agreed upon should always be followed. The key is to form proper habits and then stick with them for the long term.

- *Financial Fitness for Teens* also gave the following example for a teen to apply to all incoming money:

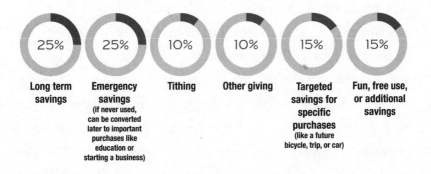

25%	25%	10%	10%	15%	15%
Long term savings	**Emergency savings** (if never used, can be converted later to important purchases like education or starting a business)	**Tithing**	**Other giving**	**Targeted savings for specific purchases** (like a future bicycle, trip, or car)	**Fun, free use, or additional savings**

- Orrin Woodward teaches his children to always put 50% of any income to savings, whether the income is 3 cents or $3,000.

- 50% to savings and at least 10% to tithing is what we recommend for most teens. But it is important to assess your own situation and work with your parents to get the right plan for you.

> **People who don't give miss out on a lot of joy in life, and they usually don't do all that well taking care of their own money either.**

This creates a powerful level of financial fitness. If you learn to do this while you are young and keep doing it, the blessings and results will be huge. People who save tend to become increasingly prosperous in their finances. People who don't almost always have money struggles.

And again, "saving" doesn't mean randomly putting away a few bills here or there. It means consistently saving a preplanned percentage of all money you get, automatically and over the long term.

Always Give

Likewise, the greatest financial leaders in the world, the ones who really get it, will tell you that it's vital to also give away some of your money. Give to tithing (your church), to charity (organizations that help people who really need it, like those who are hungry or homeless), and to philanthropy (supporting causes like literacy, freedom, great education, hospitals, etc.). This is an essential part of being wise with your money and being financially fit.

People who don't give miss out on a lot of joy in life, and they usually don't do all that well taking care of their own money either. Be a giver—to the right causes, the ones that really matter.

As a young person, be absolutely sure to discuss the money you donate with your parents—before you give. If you always do this, they can teach you what kind of giving is best, versus which kinds of giving are scams or likely be wasted or not helpful. Again, always discuss your giving with your parents.

A good amount for teens and adults to give is 10 percent in tithing and then a bit more to other good causes and needy people. Some people automatically give 10 percent to tithing and another 10 percent to other giving. This leaves them with 80 percent of what they earned, while giving 20 percent provides real blessings for many people and important purposes.

> **The greatest financial leaders in the world, the ones who really get it, will tell you that it's vital to also give some of your money.**

Other people choose to give 10 percent in tithing and dedicate 1, 3, or 5 percent to other giving. Talk this over with your parents or spouse, and make sure you do it. When you receive money, put a preplanned amount of it in your giving pile. And make sure you send that pile to the places you have chosen.

This is the first great choice of financially fit people—to always save and give whenever they earn money.

YOUTH
Call to Action

A. Make a plan that involves immediately dedicating at least 50% of any received or earned money to savings and 10% to giving.

B. Write this plan down, and share it with your parents.

C. Follow it with exactness. Never waver from it.

D. If you feel that you'd like to give a higher percentage to savings or giving, or change the 50% plan in some way, discuss this with your parents. If you agree upon a new plan, write it, and always follow it.

E. It is important to allow exceptions when a person giving you money does so for a specific purchase. For example, if your mom gives you $5 for lunch, you should spend it on lunch. Don't save $2.50 of it and only eat lunch every other day. If your grandmother gives you $900 for an art class trip to New York, don't save $450 and wait until next year. But when the money isn't specifically given for a direct purpose, follow the savings and giving guidelines you and your parents have established.

PARENTS AND OTHER ADULTS
Call to Action

1. Support your teen, and help her make her plan and follow it.

2. One of the most important things you can do as a parent is set a good example. Concerning finances, this means good habits of saving and giving. Write your own plan: Save 10% of everything you make, give 10% of everything you make, and give a little extra as well. Also, put some extra to savings until you build up at least $1,000 in an emergency fund. Then continue to build it to at least $5,000. This fund will be a huge blessing to your family and to your overall finances and feeling of security.

3. If you are an adult but not a parent, do everything outlined in Exercise 2 above.

4. Even after you have $5,000 in your rainy-day fund, keep saving the 10%, giving the 10%, giving a little extra, and saving a little extra. These are habits of wealthy people. If you follow them, never shirking, you will become much more financially fit than if you don't.

5. This preplanned percentage system is very simple. Follow it, and you'll see your finances greatly improve over time. People with sound finances follow a plan. People who don't follow such a plan always struggle financially—even if they have a high income. Every time you receive money, immediately give and save. Period.

"A fool and his money are soon parted...."

Delayed Gratification and Wise Spending

Start small.
—PAIGE HEMMIS

Be willing to give up what you want in the here and now for what you really want long term.
—CHRIS BRADY

The Big Deal

If you don't engage in delayed gratification, your finances will always be a mess. This is a very big deal in any person's attempt to become a leader and to get financially fit. You simply must use delayed gratification if you want to get ahead in life.

What exactly does this mean? Put simply: don't buy everything you want. Wisely weigh the pros and cons of every possible purchase, and always make sure that buying the thing will be more beneficial to you in the long term than saving the money.

Actually, it's okay sometimes to set aside 15 percent of whatever

> **If you don't engage in delayed gratification, your finances will always be a mess.**

money you earn and splurge with it. Sometimes the fun of just buying what you want is worth the expense—even if what you buy isn't a great value. But always limit this kind of expense to less than 15 percent of what you make.

With the other 85 percent, use delayed gratification. Is that smartphone really that valuable to you? What about the monthly payments on the smartphone? Could you do something better with that money? By using the percentages plan from the previous chapter (or something similar), you will automatically keep yourself on track.

Opportunity Cost

The phrase *opportunity cost* refers to the next best thing you could have bought if you had decided not to buy something. So let's say you really wanted the new smartphone, and it was going to cost you $130 for the phone and $65 for the monthly contract, or maybe the phone is free but you pay $90 per month for the contract.**

You've decided to buy the $130 phone and to make the $780 of payments for the next year—for a total of $910. But before you make the purchase, always ask yourself, "What's the opportunity cost?"

In other words, if you don't spend the $910 this year on the phone, what else could you buy with that money?

** By the way, which is a better deal? Always think about such things when you are considering a purchase. This is what the financially fit do. So, which of the two smartphone deals above is best? The first option will cost you $130 for the phone and $780 for the first 12 months, or a total of $910. The second option will cost you $1080 for the first year, even though the phone is free. Lesson: beware of "free" stuff. It's usually not really free. The cost is just higher in other ways. Again, think things like this through before you buy. Do this with every purchase. Not doing this is simply not smart. It's not what a financially fit person would do.

Don't just rush in because a phone looks cool. Instead, wonder if there is something a lot better that you could get with the same money.

Lesson: beware of "free" stuff. It's usually not really free. The cost is just higher in other ways.

What else could you get? Make a list. Write it down. How many dates could you take Heather**** on for $910? How many times could you go to your favorite professional soccer team's games? With just $600 of this you could go with your best friend Travis and his family to Disneyland. They've already invited you. Should you do it?

If you're an adult, could you pay down your debts by $910 and save even more on interest? Or have your emergency fund almost to the $1,000 level? Always consider what other options you have before you buy.

If you decide not to get the smartphone and go to Disneyland instead, you'll have $310 left over. But wait. If you spend $600 on Disneyland, what is the opportunity cost?

What else could you do with that $600? Or in this case, with your full $910?

It's always worth asking these kind of questions *before* you spend your money. Always. And if you earned this money, through an allowance or some other kind of work, you're going to value it a lot more than if someone just handed it to you.

So ask: What's the opportunity cost? What else could I get for this money? And if I saved it, what could I get by combining this $910 with next $300 I have to spend?

**** If you don't know a Heather, feel free to meet one and ask her out.

This kind of thinking will make you financially fit, if you keep doing it and if you're smart about your decisions.

New Words

In this chapter alone we've learned at least two new phrases that you might not have known before:

Delayed Gratification
Opportunity Cost

If you already knew one or both of them, great. If not, just look at all you're learning today. These can help you become a lot more wealthy, and at the very least more financially fit, in your life. Can you clearly define each of them?

Delayed Gratification: Putting off buying something now so that you can buy something better later.

Opportunity Cost: Making sure you're using your money for the best thing, not just the first thing that comes to mind or the shiniest thing available.

When you buy things, always put them through these tests:

1. If you wait, can you get something a lot better?
2. Can you get something better right now, instead of the item you're considering?

If you do this all the time, you'll be much smarter about how you spend your money. Over time, you'll build more savings, more prosperity, and even more wisdom. This is how leaders approach spending.

Of course, there are going to be purchases that pass both tests, and so you make them. That's great. Part of the blessing of earning money is being able to use it when you really need or want to. The important thing is to make sure you really do need or want what you're purchasing.

For example, have you ever received a gift or bought something, and it broke the next day or within a few days or weeks? That's a terrible feeling. And it feels worse if you worked hard to earn the money, and now it's all basically a waste.

Every adult reading this—and most teens—know exactly what this is like. Being a wise leader and a good money manager means that you get smart about everything you buy. Well, maybe not everything. Again, it's okay to use less than 15 percent or so of the money you just received to splurge sometimes.

But people who do this a lot soon make frustrating mistakes, and they quickly learn to slow down, think about it, and apply the lessons of delayed gratification and opportunity cost. Wise spending is an incredibly powerful tool of financial success.

The Increasing Challenge

This lesson has always separated the wise spenders from those who ruined their financial fitness by not using delayed gratification. But this is becoming even more difficult in our modern world because so many advertisers and retailers are strongly promoting exactly the opposite. Marketers are attempting to get us focused on instantaneous gratification.

The term "insta-gratification" is now a significant trend. For

> **Wise spending is an incredibly powerful tool of financial success.**

example, Apple and Google have beacon-tracking technologies so that "retailers can send you instant discount codes based on what you're browsing...."[1] Stich Fix borrows from your Pinterest Page to shop for you and send you recommendations, and Instagram allows you to buy items with a single click.[2]

All of this is designed to get you to buy before you think, ponder, consider, debate, and compare. As we said, technology is moving in the direction of another buzzword, "insta-" everthing: insta-buy, insta-makeover, insta-travel, insta-ticket, insta-care, insta-makeup, insta-stream, etc. The popular online ShopBazaar features a whole program called "Shop In An Insta." The more sellers can get consumers to skip the "think about this purchase" step, the more money they make.

Neiman Marcus even has "memory mirrors" in their stores—once you look into them, they remember your physique and sizes so you can pull up various clothing online and "compare outfits side by side with 360-degree views."[3] Your screen will show you exactly what you look like in a shirt, shoes, or other clothes, further encouraging you to buy online "right now."

Over time, these trends are becoming the norm. Various apps make it even faster.[4] But the key to your financial fitness is found elsewhere—delayed gratification and wise opportunity cost thinking. Don't be swayed by the "insta" fad.

Tom and Eric

Remember the two stories from the last chapter, one about 24-year-old Tom and the other about 12-year-old Eric? (It's pretty hard to forget these two stories, isn't it?) Based on what you've learned so far in this book, do you think Tom saves and gives each time he receives any money? What about Eric?

Of course, we can't be sure—because we don't know everything about these two young men. But from what we do know, it's obvious that Eric pays attention to financial fitness. If he understands Tool #2 (Save and Give *Before* You Spend), or Tool #3 about spending wisely, he no doubt follows them. In fact, the story specifically showed him using delayed gratification.

But what about Tom? Do you think he saves 50 percent or even 10 percent whenever he earns or receives money? And do you think he uses the tools of delayed gratification very often?

Probably not. To all these questions. But there's more. Do you think Tom frequently uses opportunity cost questions before he buys something?

Again, it seems unlikely.

On the other hand, Eric probably uses all these practices. Or at least he tries. Maybe he forgets sometimes, but it seems obvious that he does his best to be smart about money.

> The tools of wisely managing your money work *together*. When you do a few of them, it is much easier to do the rest. When you ignore some of them, it is usually more difficult to keep applying and benefitting from the others.

The Connection

All this brings up an interesting thread that runs through these important financial tools—the ones we've already covered as well as those still ahead. The tools are interconnected in a significant way. Specifically: the people who apply some of them are a lot more likely to apply the rest of them. At the same time, the people who don't use most of them are less likely to utilize any of them.

The tools of wisely managing your money work *together*. When you do a few of them, it is much easier to do the rest. When you ignore some of them, it is usually more difficult to keep applying and benefitting from the others.

Why This Is Great

In fact, this is all very good news. Apply the tools we've just covered, and everything else will be a lot easier. And the first three aren't difficult or complex. They're simple and easy:

1. Learn the lessons that come from a good allowance system, including earning your own way in life, being wise about all spending, not believing in something for nothing (entitlements), saving and giving, knowing the value of money, working hard, and forgoing purchases that just aren't worth it.

2. Every time you earn or otherwise receive any money, save and give the right predetermined amounts before you even consider spending.

3. Spend wisely, by applying delayed gratification and opportunity cost questions. Don't simply waste your money. Be smart about all purchases.

These three tools are basic. They work. They bring the power of financial fitness and sound money management into your life.

Youth can do them, and youth must learn to do them. Adults must do them too.

They are not hard or difficult. They simply require that we learn them, choose them, and apply them. The more consistently we do this, the better the results. And they work for anyone who will actively apply them.

Those who consistently use these tools usually end up like Eric or his dad, from the story above, on the path to true financial fitness and success. This is true whether you are 12 years old, 35, 74, or any other age. These tools are real. And they are effective.

YOUTH
Call to Action

A. Have a discussion with your parents about the meaning and value of delayed gratification.

B. Have a discussion with your parents about the meaning and value of the opportunity cost question ("If I don't buy this, what else could I buy with the same money?").

C. Make a plan to incorporate both of these tools into all your spending. Write it down. Show it to your parents, and discuss it.

D. How important is it to be aware of marketing strategies many companies and advertisers use to get you to buy without thinking through each purchase?

PARENTS AND OTHER ADULTS
Call to Action

1. Make a plan to incorporate both of these tools (delayed gratification and opportunity cost questioning) into all your spending. Write it down. Use it to greatly improve your finances.

2. If you are a parent, make a plan to teach both of these to each of your children. Then do it.

3. How important is it to be aware of marketing strategies many companies and advertisers use to get you to buy without thinking through each purchase?

*"Genius is one percent inspiration
and ninety-nine percent perspiration...."*

TOOL #4

Go and Find!

Spend time with wheelers and dealers....
Speak up.... Don't wait for perfection.
—LORI SANTOS

Money Doesn't Just Appear

In addition to the first three basic tools of financial fitness covered in earlier chapters, here is another vital key: If you wait for money to come to you, you'll probably be waiting a long time; the financially fit go and find it.

Perhaps Chris Brady taught this principle best when he told a story about his own family. He wrote:"In my family, my kids often come to me and say, 'Dad, how can I earn some money?'"

Please notice right off the bat that these kids are not like Tom from earlier chapters. They have obviously been taught that if they need money for something, it's their responsibility to earn it. They don't say, "Dad, I need some money," or "When can you give me some money for...?"

The begging method of demanding money from a parent often includes letting your words trail off and just hoping Dad or

Mom says, "Oh, sure. How much? $300? No problem. Here it is. Come back if you want any more."

Too many youth have learned to use just this method! Sad.

But it's clear that the Brady children have learned different lessons. They take responsibility for earning their own money and are willing and even eager to work for it. It's wonderful that they use the word "earn" in their question: "Dad, how can I earn some money?"

> **Here is another vital key: If you wait for money to come to you, you'll probably be waiting a long time; the financially fit go and find it.**

Brady continued: "To which I always reply, 'Well, I am glad you are feeling ambitious and want to earn more. However, life doesn't work that way. You don't get to just come to me and ask to earn more money, and have me dream up additional chores or jobs that I'll pay you for.

"You have to do it the way the real world works. Meaning: look around this house, yard, and property and come up with things you can do to contribute. Something you think is really needed, and that is valuable enough to propose to me. If it's worth it to me to pay for it, then you've got a deal.

"Sell me on the idea of it; we can negotiate a price and come to terms on what you'll do and how much you'll earn, and then I'll agree to pay you for that work."

Just Count the Lessons…

Brady tells us: "By the way, this has *always* worked very well in our family." This method teaches the young person to earn her own way but also to take initiative, think about needs, and use creativity and leadership. It also teaches her to make financial proposals, negotiate effectively, and then follow through.

These lessons are invaluable. They are, literally, priceless. And they are the natural lessons that come when parents use this method. Young people who learn in this way have a huge boost to their life because they learn to think like entrepreneurs and act like successful leaders. Again, this is priceless.

Moreover, this very process naturally teaches young people to start businesses. It is entrepreneurial from the get-go, meaning that young Jenny or Megan learns to be an effective entrepreneur first. If she decides to seek a job later, she automatically takes her entrepreneurial skills, wisdom, and leadership experience with her.

Compare this to the youngster who learns to do jobs first but never quite grasps important entrepreneurial lessons like creativity, initiative, ownership, etc. The leadership path is better than the followership path.

Let's learn from some examples.

Jake's Holiday

Jake sat on his couch, frustrated. He didn't even bother to turn on the television, so his mother knew he was really upset.

"What's up, Jake?" she asked. "Can I help you somehow?"

Jake looked at her, then shook his head slowly. "I don't think so," he said. "I...."

He returned to his silence.

Worried that something was really wrong, Jake's mom put down her work and walked across the room. She sat down next to him and repeated, "What's up, J?"

He sighed. He knew she would keep asking, and to tell the truth, he really did want her help, so he sat up and looked at her. "Mom, what's your favorite holiday?"

Surprised at this turn in the conversation, she tilted her head to one side and pondered. "Well, I love Thanksgiving. And I love the Fourth of July..." She laughed. "I guess we're a pretty American family, aren't we? My family's traditions all seem deeply rooted in the American holidays."

Jake nodded. "Mine too. But I think my favorite holiday is Christmas."

Mom raised one eyebrow. "Really? That surprises me. I've never heard you say that before. I guess I thought your favorite holiday was Thanksgiving. Like mine."

"It used to be," he responded. "But last year our Israeli exchange student Mike really made me think. I loved learning and doing all his holiday traditions with him. And I think he really liked ours as well. It was fun to spend the holidays doing both Christmas and all Mike's traditions."

Mom nodded. "You know, you're right. That was really special."

Jake leaned forward. "I especially loved giving him that gift— you know, the carved horse from the gallery. He loved it, and I had to work hard around the house to earn enough money for it. But it was worth it. I knew he'd take it back home with him and treasure it."

"Wow, Jake, I didn't realize that was such a big deal for you. I mean, you did work very hard to earn the money...."

"That's just it, Mom. I want to give Bobby and Erica really good gifts this year. And I want to get a good gift for you. And for Dad. But I'll need to earn more money than the jobs you have around here. I did everything there was to do in this house and our yard last year, and I'll need a lot more work to earn what I want this year."

He sat back, dejected. "I just don't know what to do."

Mom smiled. "Jake, it's not like you to mope around like this. You know what to do."

"I do?" he asked, genuinely surprised.

"Look out the window," she said as she pointed.

Jake looked. After a few moments, he turned to his mother with a questioning expression. "Uh...what?"

"What do you see out there?" she asked.

He looked again. "Um...fields. Fences. The Baxters' house and barn."

"What else?"

He looked again. "Horses in the field. That truck driving past.... I don't know what you mean, Mom. What am I supposed to be seeing?"

"We live in a farm community, Jake. There are a lot of older couples on the ten blocks that surround us, and at least a half dozen farms. What does that tell you?"

Jake just looked at her.

"How many of them have work that needs to be done right now?" she asked.

Jake's eyes immediately widened. He looked back out the window, across the fields, down the streets. "You mean, ask them for a job?"

"Not exactly," she replied. "Most of them don't want to hire anyone for a full-time position. The big jobs are already taken, and you're too young. But what's not getting done in those homes

53

and farms? I bet a lot of older couples would love to get some help moving boxes, raking leaves before more snow comes, or mending the fences around their yard. I bet you can find a dozen jobs to do, and if you work hard and don't charge too much, they'll have you back next year as well. And for many years to come, if you want."

Jake grinned. He knew she was right.

"Don't forget your coat," Mom yelled as he headed out the back door.

An Hour Later

When Jake returned, he looked more dejected than ever.

"What happened?" Mom asked.

"Well, I knocked on six doors, all neighbors. I told them I wanted to earn money for Christmas presents and would be happy to do jobs for them. Nobody had anything. Nobody. It was frustrating and cold."

Mom laughed.

Jake grinned in spite of himself. "Why are you laughing?" he asked.

"Jake, what would your dad say if you just asked him for a job here on the ranch to earn some money?"

Jake's eyes got big. "Oh, right. He'd say I need to come to him with a proposal."

"Do you think your neighbors would like that better too?" Mom replied.

"Yeah. You're right!"

"But I wouldn't go back to the people who already turned you down. Try some new houses."

Three Hours Later

"I just earned thirty dollars!" Jake called out loudly as he walked through the back door. "See…." He held it out in both hands.

Mom smiled. "Well done, son. Did it take long to get a job?"

"Not at all. I tried the Websters, by looking over their yard and asking if they wanted their woodpile chopped. They didn't, so I walked over to the Carlsons. I couldn't decide whether to propose raking their garden and cleaning out all the old corn stalks and weeds for the winter, or fixing up their old log fence that had fallen down in quite a few places—it goes all the way around their whole farm, you know.

"So I knocked on their door and proposed both. I said, 'I'm earning money to buy Christmas presents for my brother and sister, and I wonder if you'd like someone to rake and totally clean up your garden plot. Or I could go around your whole property and fix up the whole fence. Then you can pay me whatever you think my work is worth.'

"Then I just stood there for a minute, hoping she'd say yes. She grinned and called her husband. Mr. Carlson came, and I had to repeat the whole thing. I thought he was going to say no, but instead he said: 'Go clean up ten rows of the garden plot for free, and then come get me. If I like your work, I'll pay you $30 for the whole job.'

"I did it, and he liked it. So I finished it all…."

"That's great, Jake."

"But that's not the best part," Jake couldn't stop talking excitedly. "When he paid me, Mr. Carlson asked me to come back tomorrow and do the whole fence job for another thirty dollars!"

The Whole Story

Later that month, on December 25th, Jake happily watched as his brother, sister, and parents each opened a gift he had thoughtfully selected, purchased, and wrapped for them. It was as special for him as when his exchange-student friend Mike had shared his holiday traditions the year before.

But there is more to this story. Jake not only earned enough money for the gifts, he also made a lot of friends in this small town. He already knew many of the names and faces, but during this work adventure he got to know a lot of people on a much more personal level.

In fact, later that first week, a woman walked up to Jake's mom at the grocery store and asked, "Did one of your sons come by my house asking for jobs this week? I seem to recall that he belongs to you."

> **A key financial tool for anyone who wants to be financially effective is to "Go and Find."**
> **Don't just wait for opportunities to come. Actively seek them out.**

Not sure where the woman was heading with this question, Mom said, "Yes, probably. My son Jake went out looking to earn some money this week."

"Oh good," the woman said. "I turned him away when he knocked on my door, but after he left I got looking around and realized I have a lot of things I need done. All my children have married and moved away, and since my husband Vince hurt his back, I seem to just collect piles of things that a young man could help move for me. Do you think he'd still be willing to come over and help me?"

Jake started a small odd jobs business in the neighborhood and built friendships and ran service projects along with earning money. Even though his family moved shortly thereafter, the lessons he learned lasted as he grew up.

What Lessons?

Specifically, a key financial tool for anyone who wants to be financially effective is to "Go and Find." Don't just wait for opportunities to come. Actively seek them out. This is one of the most important financial and success tools parents can teach their children, and it is as easy as doing what Chris Brady outlined above:

- Teach them to *earn* the money they need, not just expect it to be given by parents or anyone else.

> **Principles apply everywhere, and they'll work in every family.**

- Teach them to look for opportunities. Really look. They'll find something. When they need money, teach them to look around, see what is needed, and make a proposal.
- Teach them to not give up when the answer is "no". Keep trying until they get to "yes".
- Teach them that good, honest, hard work will lead to more opportunities.

- Teach them that very often they'll make more money with entrepreneurial proposals and ventures than in normal chores or jobs.

As a young person, learn these lessons as soon as possible. And apply them for life.

Adults can use this same principle in many ways. When more money is needed, don't just wait for an opportunity; go and find one—see a need, make a proposal, and keep doing it until an opportunity comes.

Positives

Obviously, you don't have to live in a farm community to apply these tools. They work in every setting and situation—though of course you'll need to adjust for safety concerns, the culture of your community, and other factors specific to where you live. The principles apply everywhere, and they'll work in every family.

They'll definitely work in your own home, especially if your parents get on board.

Warnings

In some places, it isn't safe (or legal) for minors to work beyond the home. Know your local culture, and apply these tools accordingly. But these principles can certainly work in any home. Young people can learn a lot about successful financial behavior when their parents apply simple things like the Brady System of allowances and also this second Brady System of showing initiative instead of just asking for additional chores.

Likewise, young people should closely communicate with their parents when doing any work or businesses. This is extremely important. Initiative is wonderful, but always talk through such projects with your parents or guardian before doing them. And follow their advice.

For example, Carl and Luke (ages 17 and 16) were offered a job putting up festive Christmas lights on houses during one holiday season. When they consulted with their parents, Carl's mom and dad quickly agreed. But Luke's parents required that he not climb on any roofs during the project.

Later that season, Carl slipped and scraped his back. Fortunately, he had tied a rope around his waist, and this saved him from a serious fall. When he was treated at the doctor's office, insurance covered the whole expense of his minor injury.

Luke, witnessing the whole event, later asked his parents if their insurance would have covered him if he had slipped. They explained to him that no, they were uninsured at the moment and they would have had to pay for the medical expenses out of their own pocket. In fact, the cost would have exceeded the entire amount Luke made hanging Christmas lights for several weeks.

Young people should closely communicate with their parents when doing any work or businesses.

Luke was very sobered and thankful that his parents had given him the "no climbing on roofs" rule. He hadn't understood why they did this, and before the accident he considered them silly and out of touch for it. After the little fall, he realized how wise they had been.

Luke requested that in the future his parents tell him the reason for things, if possible, because it would help him learn how to make better decisions. They agreed. In fact, they realized that they should have just told him the reason from the beginning. Luke and his parents both learned important lessons from this experience.

Luke was so impressed with what he had learned that he asked Carl if his parents thought about insurance before the fall. "Yes," Carl replied. "When I first asked them about doing this job for a few weeks, my dad checked on our insurance and whether any problem would be covered. He told me it would but that I must always be as safe as possible anyway. He was more worried about my safety than about insurance, but he checked it just to be sure."

Again, the big warning about any entrepreneurial endeavor by a child or youth is to fully talk it over with your parents and discuss all issues of safety, legality, and making wise choices. Don't ever skip this lesson.

YOUTH
Call to Action

A. When you need money, don't just ask for it, and don't just ask for jobs to earn it. Look around. See real needs in your home, yard, property, etc. If your parents agree, you might also consider opportunities and needs in the neighborhood or community.

B. When you see needs, make a proposal. Think it through, and make a good case for what you want and especially for what your parents or other customer(s) will receive. Practice making a good proposal.

C. Learn to negotiate as you find and fulfill such proposals.

D. At times, consider offering to do the first little part of the work for free so the customers can see the quality of your work. Once they want you to fulfill the entire project, negotiate a fair price that is worth it to you.

E. Always (always!) do a great job as you fulfill your part of the deal.

F. Right now, set up and take part in a discussion with your parents about the main points in this chapter. Really talk about them. How can you better apply these tools right now in your life? Learn both from the wisdom of this book and the wisdom of your parents.

PARENTS AND OTHER ADULTS
Call to Action

1. Complete Exercises A and B above, for yourself. Write your answers.

2. What are you going to need to change in your life in order to ensure that you get what you want (and don't get what you don't want) in the next ten years? Write these down as well. Then do the same with twenty years.

3. If it won't cause an argument, discuss these thoughts with your spouse. If it will cause an argument, you probably need this book even more than most people do. If possible, make a plan with your spouse to read each chapter together, and gently—kindly, in positive, uplifting tones—talk together about what you are learning.

"He who hesitates is lost..."

Three Ways to Pay for the Things You Need and Want

No one holds failure against you; it's just part of the game. Today's entrepreneurial world will respect you for trying. Plus, if you've never failed, it looks as if you're playing it safe rather than trying to hit one out of the park.
—LESLEY JANE SEYMOUR

Three Forks in the Road

A poem by the famous Robert Frost tells about coming to a major fork in the road of life. Just imagine it. You've been on a certain path, and you're headed somewhere important. But now you arrive at a split in the road. One path goes off in one direction. The other path heads in a totally different direction.

Which one do you take?

In Frost's poem, the leaders take the harder path, the one less traveled, the one that leads to eventual greatness. The majority of people take the path that looks easier, but the truth is that the best path is the one that truly gets you where you want to go.

Another famous writer, Lewis Carroll, told the epic children's story of *Alice in Wonderland*. At one point during her adventure, Alice is faced with a similar choice. She has to choose between different possible paths but isn't sure which is best.

> The majority of people take the path that looks easier, but the truth is that the best path is the one that truly gets you where you want to go.

At this point, she asks the Cheshire Cat which path she should take. He answers that her decision depends entirely upon where she wants to end up. Alice responds that she doesn't know where she wants to go, and the Cheshire Cat tells her that if she doesn't know where she wants to end up, it doesn't much matter which path she takes.

The Financial Fork

In finances, there is a similar fork in the road. But instead of two possible paths, there are three main options—each leading to a different result and a different life experience. If you don't know which result you want, it doesn't much matter which road you choose.

Part of being financially fit is to know where you want to end up. As we discussed in earlier chapters, you want to have all the funding needed for your family and also to fulfill your life purpose. You want to have abundance, not scarcity. And you want to have time to fulfill your life purpose and be with your family a lot, not just live as a slave to your bills.

Even if you don't yet know what your exact life purpose will be, just knowing that you do have one, and that it will be important, can help you make the right choices. You know that you care where you end up financially, because you want to live your life purpose and give your family all it needs. This is a powerful place to start, and it leads us to some very basic but essential questions.

Three Basic Paths

If you have enough money to buy the things you need, you'll have an easier time than if you are usually broke. And if you also have enough money to buy some or all of the things you *want*, you'll be glad. If you don't have enough when you need it, or want it, you'll sometimes (or frequently) wish you had taken a different path.

To summarize: You're going to need and want to buy some things in this life, and you'll usually need money to do so. This brings us to the basic money question:

How are you going to get the money you'll need and want in life?

There are three main possible paths:

1. From a job.

    ...or...

2. From a career.

    ...or...

3. From a business.

The Paths Defined

The differences between these three paths—job, career, or business—are very important, and very interesting. To put this as simply as possible:

Job

> You get paid for your time working or for how much specific work you complete.

Career

> You get paid a salary for your work, based on your skills, knowledge, experience, background, abilities, training, education, connections, performance, etc.

Business

> You pay yourself out of the income and also the profits from the business (or businesses) you own.

Of course, sometimes people mix up these definitions. For example, people often don't clarify the difference between jobs and careers. But in general, those with careers get paid a salary—a set amount, sometimes with extra rewards and bonuses. And to get a salary, one's abilities, background, and connections are almost always very important.

Careers are generally long term, grow out of special aptitudes or abilities you bring to the table, and usually involve upward mobility or advancement as the years go by. Jobs, on the other hand, are usually just an exchange of work for pay.

Most people who work for someone else—a person or an organization—have either a job or a career. Those with jobs usually get paid either by the hour, the day, or by how much specific work they complete.

People on salary usually get paid more money than people with jobs who get paid by the hour. To keep these things as simple as we can, we use the word "career" to mean people on salary, and the word "job" for those who aren't on salary.

But there is another path, the business ownership road to making a living. All three have pros and cons, and we're going to learn what they are. Knowing this is essential if you are going to make the best decision about which to focus on in your life.

Jobs, Careers, and Business Ownership Compared: Pros and Cons

These three paths entail more than just deciding whether you'd rather be a doctor, lawyer, teacher, engineer, programmer, artist, etc. Why? Because some doctors have a job, others have a career, and still others run their own practice and are business owners as well as doctors. This same thing is true of almost every other type of work as well.

In short, this isn't about choosing your work description, such as nurse, accountant, salesman, welder, and so on. It's about deciding *how* you want to get paid:

- by the hour or by the specific work you complete
- on salary
- by yourself out of your business income and also profits

Here are some of the major, most basic, defining pros and cons:

Path	Pros	Cons
Job	*You don't have to spend a lot of time on work once you've clocked out for the day.	*Usually much lower pay than salaries or successful business ownership. *Your boss sets your schedule, the timing, and most of the details of your work.
Salaried Career	*Usually higher pay than a job. *In certain salary positions such as lawyer and doctor, there are status rewards.	*You frequently have to work very long hours, and weekends or holidays if needed. *Your boss often sets your schedule, and many of the timing and other details, and expects you to significantly exceed your official schedule.
Business Ownership	*You often get to set your own work schedule, or at least have a huge say in when you work and when you don't. And once the business is well established you can take time off if needed without losing income. *Successful business owners frequently make more money than people with jobs or in salaried careers—because they get paid for their work, and get paid again (usually much more) for the profitable success of the business. *Tax laws are generally favorable for business owners. *You can build your business(es) around your interests, passions, and life purpose. You can focus on projects you really love. As a result, many business owners deeply love their work.	*Starting and building your business takes a lot of hard work. *There is risk involved in starting and building a business, and often it can take a while to reach the point where you're making enough to get paid. *You must be able to motivate yourself on a consistent basis in order to build a successful business.

Note that nearly everyone has to work very, very hard to succeed in any of these three paths, and of course there are risks involved in all of them.

Solution: Prepare Well for
All Three Forks in the Road!

Most young people in today's world are highly encouraged to lock themselves into educational paths that direct them toward the best job or career they can find. As a result, the majority of modern youth end up selecting either the job fork or the career fork in the road. By the time they are somewhere between 17 and 24 years

Note that nearly everyone has to work very, very hard to succeed in any of these three paths, and of course there are risks involved in all of them.

old, most young people today have picked one of these two paths and are pursuing it.

For some people, this turns out to be an excellent choice. But remember the 80 percent of people in the United States who don't like their work, job, or career? Far too many people make the wrong choice when it comes to the triple fork in the financial road. And sadly, they often make a lot less money than they would if they had made a different choice.

So, let's get real. We have a different recommendation for everyone who reads this book. Instead of choosing between the three financial paths of job, career, and business ownership while you are young, consider learning how to excel in all three. Or at least keep all three open as options as you form your preparatory experiences.

This is a deep and profound thought. We estimate that less than 5 percent of young people ages 16–27 use this approach. In fact, it seems like less than 5 percent of all people make this decision.

But think about it. If you are good at all three options, if you develop your skills and knowledge in all three, you're going to have a lot more options and opportunities in your life. In fact, you may choose a job at some point in your life, a career or even more than one career at different periods of your life, and also business ownership when it suits you.

You may start in a job to get some basic cash coming in, use some of that money to get education and skills that can help you launch a career, and then use your career's salary to help fund a business you begin in the hours outside of work. This is a common path many use to ultimately become business owners, and it illustrates how you can use all three paths to get where you want to go in life.

This Is the Key

If you put all your educational and learning focus on preparing for only a job or career while you're young, and don't put any real effort into developing the skills of successful business ownership and leadership, you're just throwing roadblocks into your own future. Now, let's be clear. We believe that almost anyone can get serious about entrepreneurship at some point in life, even in his or her 50s, 70s, or older and make it happen. But it is much more effective when you've already learned the skills and wisdom of excellent entrepreneurship in your youth.

If you've already worked to become a proficient leader and team builder, you won't have to spend nearly as much time figuring these things out later when you decide to become an owner. This is very important.

The truth is, if you learn to be a successful business owner, you'll be able to use these skills in a career or job whenever you choose. But if you focus only on a job or career, it can be a massive undertaking later on in life to make the switch to entrepreneurial leadership.

For example, one business expert, best-selling author Michael Gerber, called this path in the road "The E-Myth," or "The Entrepreneurial Myth." His research shows that very few people from the job or career paths know how to effectively make the transition to business ownership. Thus, most of the people who try to make this change end up failing.

There are three possible ways to overcome this problem. **First, learn the skills and abilities of business leadership in your youth**, along with everything else that is part of your education. Indeed, this is exactly what you are doing by learning and applying the tools in this book. These tools are a powerful primer on many of the very leadership skills you'll need.

> **If you learn to be a successful business owner, you'll be able to use these skills in a career or job whenever you choose.**

Second, if and when you decide to become a business owner, work with a hands-on mentor—the kind who has already accomplished what you are trying to do and will help you do it as well. This is an essential part of effective leadership. Very few who skip this step succeed in the challenging world of entrepreneurship.

Third, just learn by trial and error. Note that this is a bad choice, but the truth is that most people who want to become business owners somehow sadly select this path. In their youth, they focus on preparing for a job or career (or just playing around), and then they work in that job and career for a few or many years. Eventually, they want much bigger pay for their hard work, or they want to spend more time with their family, or some other important issue arises that causes them to look into business ownership.

But when they try to make this shift, they realize they just don't have the entrepreneurial or leadership skills to do it effectively. Only a small percentage of people who try to make this big shift later on in life actually succeed in building a successful business.[5]

That's a big deal. But it can all be fixed by doing two things: learning the skills and habits of effective business owners and leaders (preferably in your youth), and learning how to find and work with excellent mentors. When you do these two things, you have real choices—jobs, career options, and business leadership opportunities. You can choose one, two, or all three of these paths in your life, because you are prepared. And you have kept all three doors open.

Indeed, with such preparation, if you want to shift to business ownership at some point, you have already built a foundation for success. This is a much better option than simply choosing the job or career path and ignoring the great opportunities of entrepreneurship and successful ownership. We make this point because the tendency in society and school today is to assume that all kids should follow the same path through higher education and a career. We want you to open your eyes to wider possibilities and be prepared for anything!

If You're No Longer a Youngster

Now, if you are already past your youth, and you never had the advantage of learning the skills and wisdom of excellent business ownership, you can still make the change—the key to your success will be choosing the right mentor or mentors to work with. As we already mentioned, select a mentor or mentors who are already achieving what you want to achieve and excelling at it—and who are willing to help you do it as well.

> **You're going to want and need to buy some stuff in your life. And you're going to need some money in order to do it. But how you get your money will have a huge impact on your life experience and success.**

Then listen to them and follow their guidance. It really is this simple. Of course, building a successful business isn't ever easy. But with the right mentor(s), you can do it—regardless of your age.

What to Do

Finally, let's just be honest. You're going to want and need to buy some stuff in your life. And you're going to need some money in order to do it. But how you get your money will have a huge impact on your life experience and success.

In general, a successful career can pay you a lot more than most jobs, and successful business ownership can earn you even more. It is certainly true that money isn't everything in this world, or even the most important thing. Not by a long shot. But having enough for your wants and needs and to build your family and achieve your life purpose is very important.

Most people, sadly, don't reach this objective. Many of them miss out on it specifically because they don't learn the skills and wisdom of effective business owners and entrepreneurial leaders. In fact, these same skills are incredibly helpful for those seeking to succeed in both jobs and careers, as we've said.

The tools in this book will help you learn and apply many of these very skills and principles.

To repeat: everybody has to pay for many of the things they want and need in life. But how you earn the money to pay for these things (from a job, a career, or business ownership) will make a huge difference in how much money, free time, and enjoyment you have during the journey. When you learn and apply the skills of ownership, you open up the potential of all three paths in your future. All doors remain open.

Carl's Lesson

For example: When 17-year-old Carl got home, long after dark, he sat down in the living room and put his elbows on his knees and buried his face in his hands. He sat like this for several minutes, not uttering a word.

His mom and dad continued the conversation they had been having when he came in, and his little brother kept watching the soccer game on TV.** After a while, Carl's dad noticed him, and looked over at his mother with a question on his face. She shrugged and looked at Carl with concern.

> **When you learn and apply the skills of ownership, you open up the potential of all three paths in your future.**

**Manchester United was shellacking Chelsea 3 to 0.

"Carl," Dad said, "what's wrong? You look exhausted."

Carl looked up from his hands and asked, pleadingly, "Is this what life is about? Is this what people do for their whole adult life? Go to work early in the morning, work hard all day, and then come home just in time to eat dinner and go to bed—then start the whole thing over, day after day? Is this what it means to grow up and become an adult?"

His parents glanced knowingly at each other. "Well," Dad replied, "for a lot of people this is exactly what most of adult life is like. It's called holding down a job."

Carl put his face back in his hands and just sat there. "I hate this!" he said between his fingers. "I mean, I really hate it. We've only been hanging Christmas lights for a few weeks, and I'm absolutely sick of this. I don't want to live this way. Not ever."

He looked up at his parents. "You guys found a different way to do it. Can I learn to do things like you?"

"Well," Mom said, "first of all, you need to realize that the way you are earning money and the way we've built our business are both very, very hard work. Doing it our way isn't the easy path, not at all."

She smiled. "But there really is something to be said about being your own boss. You've seen how hard we work, son. But you also know that on almost any given day, or even for a week or more, we can take time off and do something important to us. That's a huge benefit of business ownership."

"I know," Carl said. "You've taught me so many times about jobs, careers, and business ownership that I'm sick of hearing it. But today it...." He sat up straight and sighed loudly. "Can you just explain it one more time? But I only want to know how I can be a successful owner. Don't bother with the job or career stuff. I've had enough of jobs. Tell me what I need to do, starting right now, to be a really successful owner. Please...."

"First," Mom quickly responded, "it's going to be a lot of hard work."

"I'm ready," Carl replied sincerely.

The conversation lasted long into the night.

YOUTH
Call to Action

A. Discuss the pros and cons of the three paths outlined in this chapter with at least one adult who is a successful business owner.

B. After you have completed item A, discuss the three paths outlined in this chapter with your parents. Talk about the pros and cons.

PARENTS AND OTHER ADULTS
Call to Action

1. Discuss the pros and cons of the three paths outlined in this chapter with at least one adult who is a successful business owner.

2. Help your youth discuss the pros and cons of the three paths outlined in this chapter with at least one adult who is a successful business owner.

3. After you have completed steps 1 and 2, discuss the three paths outlined in this chapter with your youth. Talk about the pros and cons.

"Hitch your wagon to a star...."

PART TWO

HANDS-ON
MONEY TOOLS

"Honesty is the best policy."

TOOL #6

Your Balance Sheet

*Most people spend their whole life working for money,
all the while remaining ignorant of what money is
and how debt controls their lives.*
—ORRIN WOODWARD

Here We Go!

At this point, we're going to launch into several very hands-on financial tools. Like the mental and leadership tools that we've already covered in this book, these very practical hands-on skills in the chapters ahead are incredibly important to financial effectiveness. And they are a lot of fun as well.

As we go we want to ask you to do yourself a favor. It will only take a tiny amount of effort, but it will be a huge blessing to you. What is it? Simply this: you're probably going to read some words and terms you have never heard before, and when you do, we want you to relax and enjoy learning them.

Don't get stumped or feel even the tiniest bit frustrated with these new words. They are words people with financial success understand, and none of them is hard or complex. They're all really simple. For example, in this chapter we're going to learn a new phrase:

Balance Sheet

This is a very simple concept to understand. But some people don't want to learn new things, and they just seem to automatically turn off their brain a little bit when new words like this come up. Please don't be one of those people. It could easily reduce the amount of money you earn in your life.

On the other hand, the few new words you are going to learn can easily make you lots of extra dollars in your life—if you just take a few moments to really understand them, and then apply them throughout your life. This book will make it easy. We hope you'll take advantage of this.

The Private Lake

Okay. Let's get started with a story that illustrates what this is all about. Business leaders Chris and Terri Brady frequently enjoy taking their family out for fun times on a lake in North Carolina. Over time, they noticed that on many occasions they had the lake nearly to themselves. Other families had docks and boats as well, but the Bradys were often all by themselves enjoying the weather, the breeze, the sun and the ripples on the water.

They began to refer to the lake as their own "private" lake. They discussed this as a family, and they marveled that during regular work hours in the middle of the day, they were almost always the only ones boating on the lake. Why? Because as business owners they could pick and choose their work schedules and select times when the lake would be mostly uninhabited.

Chris once asked the children, "Why do we have a 'private' lake?"

"Because you have assets that produce cash flow, Daddy," his little girl Christine answered.

Chris and Terri had previously explained how they had worked very hard to build their business, and they had focused on turning their work hours into assets. The little girl was right. They had assets that gave them a lot of opportunities that people without assets simply didn't have.

Assets and Liabilities

This is really very simple. *Assets* are things that, if you own them, bring you more money every month, year, etc. This money coming in is called "cash flow."

That's not hard to remember. But it's incredibly powerful. If you have a lot of assets bringing you a lot of money each month, you're going to do better financially than if you don't.

> **If you have a lot of assets bringing you a lot of money each month, you're going to do better financially than if you don't.**

In contrast, *liabilities* is a word that describes things that cost you more money every month, year, etc. For example, if you own a car, it costs money for upkeep, for licensing, for repairs, for fuel, and so on. Thus the car is a liability.

Now, if you use your car to do your work, it can also be an asset. Without it you couldn't get your work done, and less money would come to you each month.

The question is: overall, is the car more of a liability or more of an asset?

It is easy to find the answer. Look at all the costs of getting and keeping the car, and all the money the car brings in, and see which is higher. If the car costs more than it brings it, it's a liability. If it brings in more than it costs, it's an asset. (Of course, some liabilities, like a car, are still necessary.)

This is so simple that you'd think everyone would understand it. But most people don't. Not really. A lot of people buy new cars using loans, and they buy the most expensive brand they can talk themselves into.

This is really a major financial problem, because when you get a loan you still have to pay for the car, and you also have to pay a lot of extra money in interest to have the loan. Sometimes young people see a person with an expensive new car and say, "They're rich."

Everything you ever buy will be either an asset or a liability.

But the truth is that the large majority of people who are financially successful avoid taking out loans to buy liabilities. They worked hard for their money, and they know that liabilities are huge money drains. For example, many of the wealthy actually buy nice used cars with low mileage, and they pay for them all at once in cash.

This saves them many thousands of dollars in interest while providing the same transportation. They buy the car at a price that makes it less of a liability, preserving their cash to be invested in assets instead.

This is a huge deal. Everything you ever buy will be either an asset or a liability.

Balance Sheet

So right now, let's outline your balance sheet. A balance sheet is a very common tool in the financial world. It is simply a way to keep track of your assets and liabilities.

You can make one on a blank piece of paper or right here on the sheet provided below. Here's what you do. Make a list of all your assets. These include anything that brings you money every week, month, or year.

The truth is, many people don't really have assets. They "kind of" have assets, meaning they can make a list of things in their bedroom, their garage, or elsewhere that they could sell—that old baseball mitt, the Star Wars card collection, three mint still-in-the-package Barbie dolls, or a Buck knife they got for their birthday years ago. Maybe even a nice gaming set.

Adults usually have things that would bring a bit more money—the old Kawasaki that still runs great and has vintage appeal, a nice baby crib that they're never going to use again, a set of tools that would bring a good price, the gold watch that is never worn, and so on. When you really look, you probably have a number of things that aren't really serving you anymore that could be turned into cash.

But most of these aren't really assets. They might be worth something in a one-time sale. But they aren't bringing you additional money every month or year. That's what *real* assets do.

However, someone who understands the tools of financial fitness would sell all (or some of) those things and turn them directly into assets. That's awesome! How do you do it? Sell them, and put every penny into savings, or use it to start a new business, or to build a business you already have. Most people would spend the cash right away. But you know better! You want to build assets!

So just start by writing down the assets you have, if any, that keep bringing you money each month or year. Put them on your Balance Sheet.

But first, here's an example:

My Balance Sheet	
My Assets	My Liabilities
-My Allowance from doing Chores	

This is what most young people have as assets. They often have the health, time and (hopefully) good attitude that allows them to earn money. But unless they use these things to actually make money, they aren't really effective assets.

Compare what many adults might put on the asset side of their balance sheet:

My Balance Sheet	
My Assets	My Liabilities
-Skills, Training, Education, Experience, Background	
-Current Job	
-Money in a Savings Account that Pays Interest	

The question is whether this person has enough assets to bring in the money needed to cover all his liabilities (all his expenses, debts, and everything else he must spend money on which would be listed on the right-hand column under "liabilities"). If so, great. If not, he'll always struggle to make ends meet—unless he increases his assets or decreases his liabilities.

Note that the chart above is the kind of balance sheet you might typically find for a person who makes his living in a job. To compare, the following is a typical balance sheet for a person who makes his living in a salaried career position:

My Balance Sheet	
My Assets	My Liabilities
-Skills, Training, Education, Experience, Connections, Background	
-Current Salaried Position	
-Money in a Savings Account that Pays Interest	
-Money in 401(k) (this is a common retirement plan used in the U.S.)	
-Other Investments	

To really get a good comparison, we must also look at a typical balance sheet from a successful business owner:

My Balance Sheet	
My Assets	My Liabilities
-Skills, Training, Education, Experience, Connections, Background	
-Current Salaried Position with the Business that I Own	
-All Profits from the Business that I Own	
-Personal Money in Savings Accounts that Pay Interest	
-Any Money I Choose to Invest into the Business I Own	
-Retirement Money I've put Aside	
-All the Items Owned by the Business I Own, Including Real Estate, Buildings, Contracts, Savings, Investments, Vehicles, and Anything Else Owned by the Business	
-The Time, Willingness to Work, Health, Skills, Training, Education, Experience, Connections, and Background of All the Employees Who Work for Me	
-Other Investments	

Clearly, there are a number of major financial advantages to the business owner path of making a living. As mentioned earlier, people on salaried careers usually have more assets than people who make their living with jobs, and successful business owners frequently have a lot more assets than both of the others.

Okay, So What About You?

But back to you. If you are a teen, it's not expected that you've earned a lot of assets yet. It's important to have a happy, healthy childhood if possible, get a good education, learn how to love and live in a happy family, and so on. At some point, when you start thinking about your future and what you want it to look like, it's important to outline your assets.

You might not have much that earns you money every week, month, or year, but it's good to know what, if any, assets you do have.

Now, fill in your own balance sheet. What assets do you have right now?

My Balance Sheet	
My Assets	My Liabilities

Again, it's okay if your list of assets is very short. It will grow, if you do the right things. The problem arises when the only assets you have as a 12- or 17-year-old are time and your willingness to work, and later these are still the only assets you have at age 25, 37, 49, 58, or even older.

It's always going to be very hard to achieve your life purpose if the assets on your balance sheet are small. The more assets you have, and the more cash flow they produce, the more opportunities you'll tend to have.

Richer or Poorer?

In fact, there's an old saying that the rich get richer and the poor get poorer. While this isn't true for everyone, it does generally happen this way for a whole lot of people. But there's a reason for this. A simple one.

Here it is: If you have assets, you have more money coming to you. If you don't have assets, you have to work harder for money than those who do have assets. And you have to keep on working in order to keep the money coming in.

That's bad for anyone who doesn't understand that they need to build assets. But it goes even deeper than that. If you have assets, like the Bradys on their lake, you can do things at times and in ways that people without assets can't. And this makes a huge financial difference.

For example, Ansel was a successful accountant who decided to start his own accounting firm and grew it into a profitable business. As the owner, he was able to hire other accountants to do much of the firm's work, while he oversaw the business's operations. Over time, Ansel began to notice something very interesting.

Whenever his employees talked about vacations, hotels, or travel, they mentioned prices for these things that seemed very high. He wondered: Why are they paying so much more than I do for vacations and trips? He decided to do a little research and find out.

> If you have assets, you have more money coming to you. If you don't have assets, you have to work harder for money than those who do have assets.

To begin, he looked up the cost of the vacations he and his wife and family had taken during the past five years. He got very specific, writing down the exact expense of all these trips and fun events. Then he asked one of his employees, a top accountant, to do the same for his family.

When he compared the two numbers, he was shocked. His employee had literally spent just under three times as much as he had.

"Something is strange about all this," he told his wife. He kept trying to figure it out by looking at how much both families had spent on airfare, hotels, rental cars, food, movies, sporting events, and other costs.

It was during this portion of his project that he realized what had happened. When he figured it out, he was amazed. It turns out that Ansel and his wife typically priced flights and hotels over the course of many months, and then chose to go on their trips on days and weeks when the prices were the lowest. His business owner mentality caused his frugality, and his business owner freedom allowed him the flexibility in his schedule.

But his employee hadn't done this. Instead, his employee and family had taken their vacations during the most expensive times of year (and apparently hadn't shopped too hard for lower prices).

"Why would they do that?" he asked himself. "It's ridiculous. They should go when things are much less expensive."

Ansel studied the exact dates of his employees' trips and vacations. The family vacations or trips were typically in early June, right after the schools let out for the summer. Then again in early August, before the next school year started. And again during Thanksgiving week, and later during the December holidays.

Suddenly Ansel understood exactly what had happened. These were the most expensive travel and vacation times of the year because these are the only times that most people can get off work. Because of the high demand on these dates, airfare, hotels and everything else cost a lot more money. A *lot* more!

Ansel realized that as an owner these were the very times that he was willing to let his employees take vacations or time off—because other businesses do the same thing at these times of the year and having all your employees in the office isn't as vital on these days.

But as an owner, Ansel could simply take vacations when he wanted—and pay a lot less, sometimes less than half or a third of the cost for what often turned out to be much better flights, better hotels, and better vacations. He realized that there is a built-in benefit to owners in the way most of the economy works. Employees simply don't get such benefits most of the time.

Summary

People with jobs and salaried careers typically trade their time and skills for money, while business owners generally

exchange their time and skills for acquiring assets that in turn bring them money.

The difference between these two ways of doing things is very big. Even though many people with salaried careers make enough money to turn a lot of it into assets, this often isn't their focus. Some of these people do it, but many of them spend most of their income on liabilities instead—or even spend *more* than their income on liabilities and add major loans and debt to their life.

In contrast, the focus of successful business owners is to *increase assets*. As time passes, those who are consistently adding assets to the list of things they own generally become a lot more financially successful than those who don't.

The most effective assets are businesses you own, which allow you to put all your profits back into the business as you choose, thus increasing your assets at much, much higher rates. If you choose the business ownership path for your work life, this is a natural. You still have to actually choose it and do it, of course, but it is the natural course for those who want to succeed as owners.

Whatever path you choose for making your living, to get ahead financially you need to build assets. Keep this clearly in mind throughout your life, and act on it every time you receive any money.

If you select the job or career path as your way of making a living, it is important to follow a wise budget and put as much as you can toward building assets. But a lot of people on these paths aren't constantly thinking about the importance of building assets. It just isn't usually the focus in job or career culture. Nor is it as easy for these people as it is for business owners, because the owners can put most of their money into their own business. (We'll talk about different types of assets later on in the book.)

But even if for whatever reason you might decide against business ownership, it is important to find good ways to build your own assets, not just spend your money on liabilities. One good way is savings. But even savings usually only pays you less than 3 percent a year (often a lot less). It's good to have some savings, certainly, but at some point you need to find other assets to build.

This process of finding ways to put your money into building assets is called investment (or investing), and we'll deal with it further in later chapters. But for now, note that one of the very best ways to invest (if you aren't already a business owner and therefore can't invest in your own business) is to start a side business. This allows you to do what the wealthy have always done, all through history: invest in your own business.

As a teen, you can seriously consider taking the business owner path in your life. Or if you decide on one of the other paths, you can still supplement it with side businesses. For example, an adult can become what's called a "weekend entrepreneur" or "evening entrepreneur," starting and running a small business on the days when not at work.

Whatever path you choose for making your living, to get ahead financially you need to build assets. Keep this clearly in mind throughout your life, and act on it every time you receive any money. Even just saving your predetermined percentage every time you get any money makes you an asset builder. Over time you can learn to increase your assets in even better ways, but always keep saving.

Remember: if you want to get ahead financially, *build assets*.

YOUTH
Call to Action

A. Clearly define, in your own words, what an asset is. Really understand this.

B. Define the difference between an asset and a liability. Explain this to your parents or someone else. Show them how everything you ever spend money on is either purchasing an asset or a liability.

C. Take the time to go back and study each of the sample balance sheets in this chapter. Almost nobody understands how important these are the first time through. Really read them closely. Compare the differences between the sample job, career, and business owner asset ledgers. If possible, discuss these at length with your parents.

D. Add your liabilities (anything that continually takes money away from you) to the sheet, and compare your assets and liabilities.

PARENTS AND OTHER ADULTS
Call to Action

1. Clearly define, in your own words, what an asset is. Really understand this.

2. Define the difference between an asset and a liability. Explain this to your spouse, mentor, or someone else. Show them how everything you ever spend money on is either purchasing an asset or a liability.

3. Take the time to go back and study each of the sample balance sheets in this chapter. Almost nobody understands how important these are the first time through. Really read them closely. Compare the differences between the sample job, career, and business owner asset ledgers. Discuss these at length with your spouse, mentor, or someone else.

4. Look at your personal Balance Sheet. Is it where you want it to be? If not, what assets do you want to add to it in the next year? Spend some time on this question, and make a plan to fulfill your goal. Then do it.

5. Add your liabilities (anything that continually takes money away from you) to the sheet, and compare your assets and liabilities.

6. Teach these principles to your children.

"Knowledge is power…."

TOOL #7

Your "Finances" Box

Take care of your finances yourself.
A huge part of being successful in life
is handling your money.
—LORI SANTOS

Do It Right Now!

You already have a piece of paper with your balance sheet on it, and you know that over time you want your list of your assets to grow. Also, you want the value of these assets to increase.

But what are you supposed to do with your new ledger? If you wrote it in this book, you can just leave it here, right? But what good will that do you? After all, how often will you grab this book, open it to the page with your asset ledger, and ponder on it?

If you're like most people, that's not going to happen very often.

There's got to be a better way.

Actually, there is. And it's easy.

Start by finding an empty box somewhere in your house. It can be a shoebox or a little bigger. If you're a teen, a shoebox is just right. If you're an adult, a box two times bigger than most shoeboxes will work best (unless you're using motocross boot boxes, in which case you're probably fine).

Anyway, you can change boxes later if you need to, so don't worry about the size of the box. Go get it, and then come back to reading this book.

Question

Did you get the box? If not, go do it.

Seriously.

No box, no reading.

Get the box, then come back and read on....

Now that You Have a Box

Great, so now you're ready.

This is a very special box. Not the box itself, of course, but rather the things you will keep in it.

Here's what to do with this box:

1. Write the word *Finances* on it with a marker pen. Use big lettering, so your little brother won't sneak into your room and take this box away when he reads this chapter five months from now and goes looking around the house for a shoebox.

2. Put your balance sheet in the box. If you wrote in this book, make a copy of that page, or write out your own copy on a blank piece of paper and put it in the box.

   Great. See, your box is already valuable. It carries your balance sheet. That's important. Whenever you check your box, you can look at the balance sheet and add to it when you bring in more assets.

3. Remember when you made a plan for what percentage of all income you'll put to savings? Well, write the plan down and put it in your box. Review it often.

4. From now on, every time you buy something, get a receipt and put it in your box.

    Yes, every time! This may seem strange at first, but it's one of the most basic and important skills of financial fitness (and business ownership, for that matter). If you buy anything, anything at all, get a receipt and put it in your box. Never, ever miss any receipt. If you do this, and never miss, it can literally save you millions of dollars in your life. This is true. But for now, just keep every receipt for everything you ever buy in this box.

    From a hamburger to a new pair of motocross boots to anything else—keep all receipts in your box.

5. Any time you earn any money, write down who it came from, what it was for, and the date you got it, and put this paper in the box. Never miss this. Always do it, for all money you ever get.

    In fact, you may want a piece of paper especially dedicated to this. Draw a line down the middle and put "Income" at the top of the right column, and "Out Go" at the top of the left column. Everything from Step 4 above goes in the right column, and everything from Step 5 goes in the left column. You can call this your "**personal income statement**."

6.   Whenever you put anything in the box, move your balance sheet to the top of the pile. Periodically look these items over, and update them when you add more assets, spend or earn money, etc. Keep these at the very top of the papers in the box.

That's it. That's your box. It's a powerful tool for financial success, and it's very important that you do it. Now, and from now on. Always.

If you do this, you'll be learning and applying one of the most essential skills of money. Always keep track of all your income and all your expenses, on your personal income statement. And have a receipt showing them. And always show your assets and liabilities on your balance sheet.

This is vital.

All it takes is a box, and for you to always put a receipt into the box every time you make money or spend anything—and keep your balance sheet and personal income statement up to date.

YOUTH
Call to Action

A. Get a box as assigned in this chapter, and do all six things with it as explained.

B. Keep doing them long-term.

C. Show your new "Finances" box to your parents, and discuss what you're doing with it. See if they're willing to do it with you (their own box) for a few months.

PARENTS AND OTHER ADULTS
Call to Action

1. Get a box as assigned in this chapter, and do all six things with it as explained.

2. Keep doing them long-term.

3. Teach your youth this tool. Make it fun!

4. Try out the "Track and Save" app available at lifeleadership .com/subscriptions/TrackandSave. This app does the same kind of tracking outlined here, but with a cool smartphone simplicity and also coupons that can save you a lot of money. (But let the kids stick to the box! They need to learn the rudimentary financial lessons it teaches.)

"Little strokes fell great oaks...."

Your Business Income Statement

Never depend on single income.
Make investments to create a second source.
—WARREN BUFFETT

"You're Not Financially Free; You're Broke!"

Successful business owners Dan and Lisa Hawkins taught their children: "We have a lot of opportunities for you that we never had as kids, because we have built a business and have assets." But they are careful to point out to the kids: "Mom and Dad have built up assets, so we're financially free. You guys haven't built up assets yet, so you're not financially free. You're broke!"

Fortunately, Dan and Lisa are also teaching their children how to build assets, so they can choose not to stay broke as they grow up.

The truth is that the majority of people in North America, and beyond, are broke. If next month's paycheck doesn't come, they won't be able to pay their bills. If no paycheck comes for two or more months, their savings will quickly disappear.

For most people, their only financial asset is their current job or salary (and that's not really a true asset). If they lose it, they'll soon be broke. Many will be broke immediately. In fact, add the amount of debt that most people are carrying, and they are broke before they even get their paycheck. Their bills and debts are much higher than their income.

There is one way out of this. Ask Christine Brady what it is, and she'll tell you in one word: "Assets." Ask any of the Hawkins kids, and they'll say the same thing.

Assets, assets, assets.

This is the key to financial fitness, and ultimately to financial freedom.

But You Have to Act on It!

Yet most people don't act on it. As a result, they increase their liabilities over time and decrease their assets. This is exactly the wrong path.

In truth, the Brady and Hawkins children have a powerful asset that can make all the difference. What is it? A very important level of financial wisdom.

> **Anyone who knows this and acts on it consistently will become financially fit and financially successful.**

Specifically: They know that assets are the key.

Anyone who knows this and acts on it consistently will become financially fit and financially successful. Anyone who doesn't act on it will become financially flabby, and probably stay broke—or worse, get into major debt as well.

The power of understanding that assets are the key is almost impossible to overstate. It makes a huge, huge difference.

Lester's Change

For example, Ty went to school in a small town where the major industry was working for the government—the Health Department, the schools, the police, the city or county government, the Transportation Department, and so on. The big buildings in town were all government buildings. The middle-sized buildings were churches. The little buildings were houses.

Teachers, coaches, and church youth leaders mostly worked for one government agency or another, and all of them told Ty that the way to success was to get good grades, choose a practical major in college, and then get a steady government job after graduation. Ty accepted that this was the norm. After all, both of his parents had done this as well.

During his elementary years, Ty was often in classes with a young man named Lester. Many of the kids picked on Lester because he always wore the same sleeveless, dark blue, puffy hunting-style vest. He wore it during the fall, the winter, the spring, and the summer. Nobody knew for sure why Lester always wore his vest, but he did.

As he grew older, Lester still came to school with the same vest. He clearly got new ones when he outgrew the old ones, but the new vests were always the same color, style, and brand. Lester wore the same kind of vest from kindergarten through twelfth grade. Every day.

Lester also got picked on because he came from the poorer part of town. None of the kids knew what his dad or mom did for a living, but then they didn't really know that about most of the other kids either. Everyone assumed his dad had some kind of government job, like everyone else. Once in a while his dad would attend a school event, always wearing his own sleeveless, puffy vest. But for some reason the dad's vest was always dark orange.

Ty became so used to Lester that he basically forgot to notice him. He became part of the background of Ty's life, one of the things most young people don't really think about—like streets, trees, etc. The years passed.

Ty got good grades, went away to college and majored in a practical topic. Everything was on track. Then one day something dangerous happened. He noticed a flyer advertising a new science group on campus. Ty was intrigued, and he went to their weekly meeting.

He liked what he saw, and he joined. Over time, he fell in with the science group and decided to switch majors. He studied biology and really liked it. Ty's parents were very worried about him. Biology wasn't considered very practical. In fact, for many of the government workers in his small hometown, it was only valuable if you also got a teaching credential. Otherwise, in their opinion, it was a major waste of time, money, and potential.

"Most schools only need one biology teacher," his father warned him. "And a lot of them just get the football coach to teach biology. I've heard that most people with a biology degree end up working construction or on the road crew. You can do better."

But Ty stuck to his plan and his major. After Ty graduated, he went on to graduate work and eventually became a celebrated professor and speaker. One day he travelled to speak at a university far from his home, and after his speech he greeted and shook hands with a number of the participants.

After saying good-bye to a well-dressed couple, he looked up to see the next man in line. "I enjoyed your speech," the man told him. "Do you remember me?"

Ty was stumped. The man did look sort of familiar. "I'm not sure," he said tentatively. "Should I?"

The man chuckled, and replied, "Probably not. But you asked for donations in the last part of your speech, to help spread quality biological sciences in our nation. I want to help." The man handed Ty an envelope. Clearly it was a donation to the cause.

Ty glanced at the man. He was dressed like a successful businessman. The man's shoes were expensive and polished. All in all, he appeared to be a man of means and some status. He carried himself with confidence and poise. And he wore a dark orange tie.

"Thank you," Ty said.

The man grinned. "You still don't recognize me, do you?" he asked.

"I'm sorry," Ty said, "I really don't. Who are you?"

The man just laughed. "I really appreciated your remarks tonight," he said. "I'm happy I can help a little with your project." Then the man shook Ty's hand and left.

Ty put the envelope in his briefcase and kept speaking to people in the line. In his hotel room after the event, he looked through the donations in his briefcase. It had been a good night with lots of donations, and he was happy for the science foundation he was supporting.

Then he thought of the man with the envelope and looked back through the donations to see if he could tell which of them was his. When he saw it, he could hardly believe it. The name on one of the checks was that of his old schoolmate Lester.

"Lester? With the blue vest?" he asked himself out loud. He was incredulous. "No way! That can't be the same guy."

A little research online proved that it was in fact "the same guy." Lester was now the owner of a successful clothing importer, one he had built from the ground up. It specialized in colorful vests for hunting and other outdoor sports.

> No matter where you come from, how much money you have or your parents have, or what kind of situation you grew up in, how old or young you are, or what benefits or disadvantages you have, building assets will increase your financial future.

Ty sat back on his bed and smiled, remembering the high quality three-piece suit Lester had been wearing at the event. Wool, pin-striped, dark navy blue. "Nice vest," he said to the empty room. But he meant it. It had been a very, very nice wool vest. He grinned at the irony of the two kinds of vests, so many years removed from each other.

Suddenly he sat straight up, remembering the dark orange, silk tie. "It was the same color as his dad's old vest. Wow!"

Ty sat in silent amazement. Things had really changed for Lester.

Assets are powerful. If you build them, it will drastically change your life. No matter where you come from, how much money you have or your parents have, or what kind of situation you grew up in, how old or young you are, or what benefits or disadvantages you have, building assets will increase your financial future. It is that important.

What to Do Next

At this point, let's get very practical for a few minutes. Now that you've got your written plan to put a specific percentage of all money you make into savings, and you're doing it, and now that you've got your balance sheet and your personal financial statement in your finances box, and now that you put a receipt into your box every time you get or spend money, you're ready for the next step.

This is exciting. You're learning some of the most important habits and skills of financial fitness, and you might not even realize it yet. Whether you are teen or an adult, this is big-time. You're gaining the tools of financial success. Congratulations!

Now, on the last day of every month, or on the first day of the month if you prefer, go through all the receipts for the last 30 days, and write a note on them. (Or you can do this right at the time of purchase for everything you buy.)

That's right. Write a note on them. This is going to be a major game-changer for you. Most people with jobs and careers don't do this very often (unless they're accountants or bankers, for obvious reasons), but almost all business owners do this a lot. Or at least, they did it when they first started building their business.

And knowing how to do this matters. Doing it will change the way you think about money. It will change the way you spend, and the way you don't spend. Because writing a note on every receipt for all expenses and income will train you to think like an owner. And this is one of the great, hidden, key tools of financial success.

Specifically, on every receipt, write the word *Personal* or *Business*. If the expense is for your business, write *Business* on it. If not, write *Personal*. You can even abbreviate it to *B* or *P* if you like. This is important because in the world of finances it is essential to keep separate all of your business records from your personal records.

This is a powerful tool. It gets you thinking like an owner because you'll learn that when you spend money on a *B* expense, it is worth more than when you buy a *P* item. Over time, you'll start rethinking purchases before they happen: "Will this help my business? Or is it just personal? I know I need some personal expenses, but can I skip this one and build my business? After all, my business is an asset. And assets are key to financial success."

You probably won't go through these very words in your mind each time you have the chance to buy something, but your mind will start working this way. You'll frequently value *B* expenses more than *P* purchases, because you'll see that they're building assets.

This is powerful. People who see the world this way are naturally going to build more assets than people who've never even considered it. And let's be honest, most people in the world have never, ever considered this.

Business Income Statement

The next thing is to tally your receipts. What does this mean? It's very simple. When you finish writing *B* or *P* on all your receipts each month, do one more thing. Get out a piece of paper and list out all your *B* expenses and income. You've already been keeping a personal income statement as instructed in the previous chapter. Now we're going to do the same thing for your business. Here is an example:

Lemonade Stand Business Income Statement			
Date	Description	Expense	Income
Feb 6	Ike's Paper Store, posterboard and flyers	$10.61	
Feb 3	Verizon, keep track of all my flyers, make marketing calls	$46.14	
Feb 8	Walmart—lemonade and cookie supplies	$55.18	
Feb 10	Sold lemonade and cookies at rummage sale		$94.50
Feb 11	Paid my little brother for his help	$11	
Feb 11	Return unused supplies to Walmart	-$9.76	
Totals		$113.17	$94.50

This is a very simple summary, called a spreadsheet, and it's easy to do. You can do it by hand, or you can do it on the computer. Spreadsheet software is easy to find and use. Most computers already have it. The key is to list all expenses, all income, and total each of them. (Note: Do this only for your business-related activities. You are already keeping a personal income statement for your personal activities.)

This tells you how successful your business was financially.

Of course, spreadsheets can be even simpler than this—or a lot more complex and detailed. As you enter all your receipts into the spreadsheet, you have a very clear picture of what you spent and what you earned.

This is your business income statement. You have the spreadsheet for the month and the receipts to back it up. And they're all in your box.

Remember that you put all your *B* expenses and income on the business income statement, and all the *P* expenses on your personal income statement.

Repeat the process every month or continually as you go.

A Funny Thing

If you are part of a family in which business ownership is the norm, and you were a teen during the time your family was just starting and building the business, this might seem totally normal to you. "Doesn't every kid learn this?" you are probably asking.

> **Receipts and spreadsheets are part of the DNA of financial success. Successful business owners understand them.**

If, on the other hand, your family culture was not all that entrepreneurial, or it started and built up the business before or after your teen years, you likely look at this and think, "Why should kids learn this? This is crazy. What a bunch of meaningless numbers."

But they're not meaningless. Receipts and spreadsheets are part of the DNA of financial success. Successful business owners understand them, and even after they've built the business to the point that accountants handle these details, successful business owners still understand these specifics—because they learned them from scratch. Or if not from scratch, from a parent or mentor who taught them to do this when they were young—or from finance courses in college.** Again, this is a very simple system. If it seems hard, it's only because you may not have spent a lot of time doing it. But changing this can drastically improve your life. It's really quite easy. To repeat:

1. Keep all receipts, of income and expenses (if you lose or forget a receipt, write one up to replace it).

2. Mark each receipt *B* or *P*. As the business grows, you'll have separate business and personal checks, credit cards, etc., and you won't have to do this step. But you'll still have to check to ensure that you don't mistakenly buy a personal expense on a business account—or vice versa.

3. Tally up all business expenses and income on a spreadsheet, called an income statement, or handwrite it on paper. And do this often. This is how business owners keep close track of their finances.

    By the way, the Financial Fitness app called Track and Save can help you with this. It allows you to snap a picture of each receipt on your phone and keep them all in an easy digital format. Then when you tally them each month, it's faster and easier. With the Track and Save app you can track both personal and business expenses, establish a monthly budget, print data for monthly and yearly totals, and much more.

**Balance sheets and income statements are two of the most important tools for business, no matter how large (or small) the enterprise. Amazon, Apple, Tesla and almost any large company you can name are all managed using these exact same tools.

It just makes the whole process easier. It also offers many coupons that will provide huge savings each month. (Find more details at lifeleadership.com/subscriptions/TrackandSave.)

That's it. If you learn this as a teen, you're always going to know how to think in terms of assets versus wasting money. And you'll know how to read and understand basic business numbers. It will simply become natural to you. If you're a parent, teaching this to your teens is invaluable. It will greatly increase their financial wisdom.

Indeed, some educators believe that this is the kind of math that is most important to teach to youth. When the student grows up, she will definitely use it nearly every day of her life, if she becomes financially successful. This model is one thing that many of the wealthy teach their children, but most of the middle and lower classes do not. This adds to the rich getting richer and the poor getting poorer.

If you're an adult and you've never done this, start now! Do it for a year, and you'll see your financial skills rapidly increase.

Positives

Learning to maintain balance sheets and income statements is a crucially important skill. It can make all the difference. In fact, those who never learn to read numbers seldom become financially successful. They just don't have the basic skills.

> **Young people (and adults) who consistently keep all their receipts and learn to tally them in spreadsheets gain many of the most important skills of entrepreneurial and financial success.**

Yet it can be learned so easily. So simply.

Again, if you are an adult and this isn't part of your experience in life, don't knock it. It will help your kids skip many of the worst financial challenges you may have faced, and help them avoid a lot of the financial mistakes most people make. This is powerful stuff. And you should do it too. It will only help you upgrade your financial skills.

Warnings

Of course, don't just turn your small business or even side-business finances over to your 14-year-old and say, "Good luck!" You can only teach them what you actually already know. If you've never maintained accurate balance sheets and income statements yourself, do it for a while—at least a year or two—before you delegate it to someone else. (The teens can certainly help you while you're doing it.)

And when you do delegate, check the numbers very closely. Most top business executives as well as smaller business owners very carefully look over and analyze their company numbers at least monthly—and many do it almost daily or weekly. Doing the simple system outlined above will teach you the importance of financial numbers, and this can make all the difference in your financial successes.

Of course, the examples featured here use very basic numbers. If you keep building a business, you'll learn more details as things grow. But the basics will always be important.

YOUTH
Call to Action

As outlined in this chapter, create a system to help you maintain an income statement every month. Put it on a spreadsheet (or other financial software), either on a computer or just written out on a piece of paper. Keep a detailed monthly record by never missing a month. This practice will greatly help you in the future!

PARENTS AND OTHER ADULTS
Call to Action

1. If you've never done this before, do the Youth exercise above. Do it for the next year. It will make a huge difference in your life. (You can do this at the same time your youth are doing it, if you choose.)

2. If you have already done this, excellent. Find effective and fun ways to teach this to your children.

3. Spend some time carefully studying and analyzing the Lemonade Stand business income statement of expenses and income in this chapter, and discuss the details with your children. For example, do the numbers show that this is a good business plan? Or a bad one? Specifically: is it making money or losing it?

4. What happens to the numbers if you take the mobile phone expense off the list? Should the phone be on the list? Discuss the difference between considering the phone a business expense while only using it for this one day of running a lemonade stand, versus using it consistently on a lot of business ventures over the months and years.

"Make haste slowly...."

TOOL #9

Your Budget

If you don't do something different,
you'll end up where you're going.
—ORRIN WOODWARD

Tom Gets an Opportunity

"I don't know what to tell you," 24-year-old Tom said to his landlord, Trent. "I'm doing my best. I just sold my Camaro, and she was the love of my life." He shook his head sadly.

"My dad stopped giving me money to make the payments, and I didn't even have enough for food. I had to sell her. And now, I'm just not able to pay the rest of the rent. The half I just handed you is all I have. I'm sorry. I'll get you the rest as soon as I can."

"Do you still have a job?" Trent asked.

"Yes, I'm still a waiter at Denny's. It's the only job I could find. Like I said, I'm doing my best. I wouldn't blame you if you just kicked me out. But if you'll just give me two more weeks, I'll put every dime toward the rent until it's paid up."

Trent looked soberly at Tom. "Actually, I'm impressed that you sold your Camaro, and I'm impressed that you came to me on the first day of the month with half the rent. Most tenants who are struggling this much just avoid me."

"I'll be straight with you, I promise," Tom said.

"Okay, and I'll be straight with you. The rent is due on the first. I'll give you until the 15th to pay the rest, and by next month I want the full payment on the first. Are we clear?"

"Yes. Very. Thank you," Tom replied.

"Hey, before you go…." Trent's voice trailed off.

"What?"

"Actually, I'm not sure you'll care, but maybe this can help. I'm building a business, and it includes selling people a Financial Fitness program that teaches people to get out of debt and get their finances on track. If you're interested, I could show you a video and explain how it works."

"I'm interested," Tom said. "But would it interfere with my work hours at Denny's? Without that job I'll be even more broke."

"No, you read the book and listen to the audios on your own schedule. If you don't mind me asking," Trent asked, "why are you working at Denny's? I thought you were a musician."

Tom sighed, then smiled. "I am a musician, and I play Wednesday nights at the Tambor—do you know it?"

Trent nodded.

"But I only get paid tips. And while I'm trying to get a break in my music career, my finances aren't doing very well."

Trent rubbed his chin. "Actually, I think the Financial Fitness program could really help you. When can we meet and talk about it?"

"Right now?" Tom asked. "I really need help on this. And I'm done with work today...." He hesitated. "Or would you rather meet another time?"

"No, now's great. I'll grab the video and meet you down at your apartment in five minutes. Sound good?"

"Perfect."

Budgets Aren't Scary or Hard

Remember Tom almost demanding that his dad send him $850 for his car payment several chapters ago? It turns out he's not that bad a guy after all. He's learning. He's trying. He's seeking ways to get ahead.

The thing is, a lot of people with financial struggles are actually really good people. They just don't know or follow the tools of financial fitness. Or in some cases, they just hit a rough patch and need time to fix things, or they've recently started on a path to financial fitness, and they're still struggling from past challenges.

The next tool we're going to tackle is exactly what Tom needs, and it's exactly what you need. How do we know? Because it's exactly what everyone needs. Even if you're already following it, you still need to keep at it. If you quit, your finances will take a nosedive.

We're talking about a budget.

Don't Worry

Budgets are important. But for some reason, the word _budget_ feels negative to a lot of people. They get scared when they hear it, like when they hear the words _pop quiz_ or _test_. But you can just skip the scary part, because we're here to tell you that the right kind of budget isn't scary or hard. The right kind of budgets are simple, and they're easy.

And by the time you've completed this chapter, you'll probably be part of the 5 percent or so of people who really like budgets and understand how they're supposed to work. Budgets are kind of like a machine that you put to work to make sure you handle money the right way, so that you can have more of the things you really want in life. Sounds great, right?

The Best Budgets

So let's jump right in. First of all, you've actually already done your budget.

"I have?" you ask. "When? What is it? Where?"

When you outlined the preestablished percentage of everything you make that will go to savings, you started your budget. As you'll remember, if you're a teen, we recommended that you save at least 50 percent of all money you earn or receive, but we told you to talk it over with your parents and choose the right percentage for you. And we added that you should give some to tithing and charity or philanthropy.

Remember that? Well, that was a basic form of a budget. It wasn't extremely detailed like some budgets, but it was a good, solid budget. If you are still following that plan, you're already following a budget.

A budget is simply a preplan for how to allocate your income. Giving a percentage to tithing and good causes and putting 50 percent (or whatever percentage you decided upon) of all your income to savings is a budget. If you're doing it, congratulations!

Good job! You're on the path to financial fitness and great money management. Keep it up. You're using an excellent budget.

A budget is simply a preplan for how to allocate your income.

If you stopped following it, for any reason, you're sadly off your budget. Get back on it immediately. Don't let anything stop you. Follow your budget. This is very important, at least if you want to be good with money. Remember, a budget is a machine that works for you. But it only works if you'll start it up and keep it running.

A Little Deeper

Now that you are on a budget, with 50 percent (or whatever percentage you chose) of all your income going to savings, let's improve your budget a little bit more. If you're an adult and you're putting 10 percent or more of all your income to savings, the same principles apply.

To begin, go out of your way to keep all your budgeting as simple as possible. Don't overthink it. Don't worry about having some advanced budgeting software or taking a budgeting class. Just do the simple basics.

Here's what "the simple basics" are:

A Fantastic Sample Budget

1-Give 10% of all money you earn or receive to tithing.

2-Each time you bring in money, give a little to good causes that help needy people or make a positive difference in the world.

3-If you are a child or teen, put 50% of all money you earn or receive into savings, and leave it there. If you are an adult, put at least 10% of all the money you bring in to savings.

4-If you are an adult, put a little more each time you bring in money to a special emergency fund and build it up to at least $1,000. Once you have done this, keep adding to it until you have at least $5,000.

5-If you are a teen, simply figure out how to pay all your other bills and buy the other things you want with the money left over. If you don't have enough, you can either not buy some of the things you want, or you can find ways to increase your income.

Note that your business budgets, if you become an owner, will become more detailed and complex than this, but you'll naturally learn how to manage them if you're using the receipt box and spreadsheet system discussed earlier.

6-The truth is that #5 above is a pretty good budget even for adults (figure out how to pay all your other bills and buy the other things you want with the money left over). If this were all you ever did, and you kept doing it long term, it would be a good budget and greatly help your financial fitness. You'd simply have to figure out how to pay all your other bills and buy the other things you want with the money left over after paying your 10% to tithing, a little to charity, 10% to savings, and a little to your emergency fund. And if you don't have enough, you can either not buy some of the things you want, or you can find ways to increase your income.

For adults, there is a more specific budget planning outline in the *Financial Fitness Workbook.*[1*] We highly recommend it. But even when you use it, don't let it take over from the simple budget outlined here. Items 1–6 above are the most important part of your budget, no matter what other details and specifics you add in.

If you need more complexity, get it. But keep applying 1–6. They are the core of any successful personal/family budget.

7-For adults: If you still need serious budgeting help after doing everything in items 1–6, try this approach (while still following 1–6): List every item you'll need to spend money on each month, and write each item on the outside of an envelope. (You'll have an envelope for "tithing," one for "savings," one for "rent" or "mortgage," one for "food," one for "utilities," and so on.)

When you get your paycheck, cash it and put the right amount of money in every envelope. Then use your money for what the envelope says it is for. Period.

The same day, take the savings envelope to the bank and deposit your savings money. Or better still, have the savings amount directly deposited to your savings account before you get your paycheck.

When the rent or mortgage is due, take the money out of the rent or mortgage envelope, and pay the rent or mortgage. Be smart about the food envelope, and don't use it all up too fast. Once it's gone, it's gone.

Be very specific, never steal from one envelope for another, and keep to your budget. If you still can't make ends meet, you'll need to increase your income or cut any nonessential expenses you can find.

This is very simple budgeting, and it really works: As long as you stick to it and never steal from any of the envelopes to use the money for anything else. If you have extra left over in an envelope, keep it there for next month.

(It's wise to include an envelope labeled "Whatever" and put a little in it each month.)

Eighteen Months Later

"Hi Dad, it's Tom. How are you doing?"

"Wow, I'm glad you called." Dad paused for moment. "I was surprised to get your check in the mail. I never expected you to pay me back for all the money I gave you. Plus interest. I just couldn't believe it. It made me really happy—not because of the money, but just because it seems like you're really getting things in order in your life. That's great."

"It is. Things are going well. I'm still performing a lot, two or three times a week now. And I'm building my music business and really working hard at it. The Financial Fitness program I told you about taught me how to go on financial offense and start growing my own business, and I'm now teaching a lot of guitar lessons. It's also taught me how to keep a simple budget so I do better with my money. I've reached the point where I'm paying all my bills on time, have paid off all my debts, and I'm seeing my income grow each month. It's very exciting."

"That's great," Dad replied. "I'm so happy for you. Do you think you'll drop the performances and just focus on your guitar-lesson business?"

Tom laughed. "No. I still love performing, and I'm going to keep at it until I live my dreams. I know that a key part of my life purpose is to help bring people to God through the musical talents He gave me. But the lessons are helping me do my music a lot better—not just because I can pay my bills but also because my business is teaching me about what it takes to really earn success. I'm starting to apply this to my music career, and I know it's going to make a major difference."

"That's really great. I like the way you sound—so happy, so engaged."

"Well, it's not easy.." Tom chuckled. "But I have a really good mentor, and he's helping me make it all work. Like I said, it's hard work. But I'm excited about my progress."

"Do you still have that expensive car?" Dad asked.

Tom laughed again. "No, I sold that a long time ago. Hardly got anything after the buyer took over the payments. I replaced it with a little beater car. Then it broke down, and I got another old junker. I probably don't look very cool driving around the city in it, but it's transportation. It gets me to all my students and performances, and that's all I ask."

Dad shook his head slowly. "Tom, you just sound so different now. You've…changed. A lot, I think."

"I hope so," Tom answered. "Hey Dad, I really want to apologize for being such a jerk before. I can't believe I acted that way. You were so helpful and so giving. And I took it all for granted. I've learned not to be that way, and I won't do it again."

His dad didn't answer for a long moment. When he finally regained his composure, he quietly said into the phone, "Thanks for that, Tom. I'm really proud of you."

YOUTH
Call to Action

A. Why is having a complex budget often a bad idea?

B. Write out the following budget and put a copy of it in your finances box:

MY BUDGET

1. Give 10% of all money I earn or receive to tithing.

2. Each time I bring in money, give a little to good causes that help needy people or make a positive difference in the world.

3. Put 50% of all money I earn or receive in savings, and leave it there.

4. Pay all my other bills and buy the other things I want with the money left over. If I don't have enough, I can either not buy some of the things I want or find ways to increase my income.

5. I understand that my business budget will become more detailed and complex than this personal budget as my business grows, but I'll naturally learn how to manage it by using the receipt box and spreadsheet system and keeping it up to date every month.

Add any other helpful details that you want to be part of your budget.

C. Follow this budget.

PARENTS AND OTHER ADULTS
Call to Action

1. Why is having a complex budget often a very bad idea?

2. Write out the following budget and put a copy of it in your finances box:

MY BUDGET

A. Give 10% of all money I earn or receive to tithing.

B. Each time I bring in money, give a little to good causes that help needy people or make a positive difference in the world.

C. Put at least 10% of all money I earn or receive in savings, and leave it there.

D. Put a little each time I bring in money into a special emergency fund and build it up to at least $1,000. Once I have done this, keep adding to it until I have at least $5,000. If I spend any of this for an emergency, quickly replenish it.

E. I also need to plan how to pay all my other bills and buy the other things I want with the money left over. If I don't have enough, I can either not buy some of the things I want or find ways to increase my income.

   Outline this plan and follow it.

F. If and when I become a business owner, I understand that my business budget will become more detailed and complex as my business grows, but I'll naturally learn how to manage it by using the receipt box and spreadsheet system and keeping it up to date.

3. Follow this budget.

4. Read and study the budgeting portions of the Financial Fitness Workbook available at Life Leadership. Use this to update and expand your budget, as needed.

5. If needed, consider using the envelope budgeting system outlined above in this chapter.

6. Keep it simple!

7. Always follow it!

8. Teach your children to follow a budget like the one outlined in the Youth section above, but personalized for their individual needs.

"Necessity is the mother of invention...."

TOOL #10

Your Savings Accounts and CDs

Many people are more enamored with their credit-based lifestyle than with true wealth creation.
—CHRIS BRADY

How to Do It

So you've been saving a predetermined percentage of all money that comes to you. Or if not, you're starting right now. You know that this habit creates assets, and this is essential to any financial success you want to have.

In fact, maybe as a teen when you first read the chapter about savings, you talked to your parents, went to the bank, and opened a savings account. Or perhaps your parents had already opened an account in your name years ago. All good.

But what if you don't have a savings account in a bank? What should you do? First, talk to your parents and ask for their help to open an account. If you're not an adult, you'll need a parent to cosign on your savings account anyway.

Before you go to the bank, you'll need some money to deposit into your savings account. It doesn't have to be very much. If the amount you have saved is less than $50, it's probably best to just use a piggy bank or put it in an envelope and keep it in a safe place in your room.

In fact, it's always important to keep at least some of your savings close to you this way. Even when you are putting much of your savings into your accounts at the bank, it's good to keep some cash on hand in a safe place in your home. Talk to your parents about how much cash to keep. But don't spend it.

Seriously, the main thing about this is to keep your savings as savings. That's what makes it savings. Don't spend it, or it won't be savings anymore!

Once you have more than $50 saved, it's smart to open a savings account at a bank. This will give you a place to help build your savings into some serious assets. Using the same bank as your parents often makes things simpler for everyone.

At the Bank

When you walk into the bank with you parents, it's all very easy. Tell one of the bank employees that you want to open a savings account, and they'll help you with all the details. It typically only takes a few minutes.

They'll most likely give you a little ledger booklet that will allow you to record the future deposits you make. Put this booklet in your finances box and update it with all deposits you make—just write them in each month when you do your receipts.

Every time you make a deposit in person, the bank will give you a little paper showing how much you deposited. This is called a deposit slip. Keep all of these in your finances box as well. It's also smart to write on each slip what the money was for, such as "June Allowance Savings" or "June Lemonade Stand Savings." Just write on the slip in pen right there at the bank when you make the deposit.

Of course, a lot of people prefer to make deposits electronically by phone, tablet, or computer. When you do this, be sure to save your transactions, and then pull them up and record them each month when you update your personal income statement.

The main thing is to always put your prearranged percentage into savings every single time you make money. This is what makes the whole thing work. And it builds assets for you.

And guess what? That's about it!

It's very simple.

A Few More Details

But before we move on, let's learn a little bit more about savings accounts that will help you as you make financial decisions over time. There are three major types of savings accounts:

- **Regular Savings Accounts** are very, very basic. You put money in. The bank keeps it in your name, paying you a tiny bit of interest to keep your money there, and you can withdraw the money when you choose. (Unless something drastic happens in the nation or the economy, like a depression or crash. This is why you always keep some of your savings in cash at home.)

  One of the main benefits of having your account with the bank is to keep your savings in a separate place so it's easier to avoid spending it. Such accounts also provide a place for your savings to grow, apart from your other financial activities.

Not all banks will use the term "regular savings account." Many banks have special names for such accounts, used only by their company. But if you tell them you want a basic savings account, they'll know what you mean.

The biggest downside of regular savings accounts is that the amount of interest they pay you is extremely small. When you are just starting, that's okay. The savings account allows you to store and build your savings over the months and years. But when you've amassed more than $5,000, for instance, in your savings account, it will be time to transfer some of your money to other places. We'll discuss this later.

Another problem with savings accounts occurs when some banks charge fees if you go below a certain amount on deposit. Ask about this when you set up your account, before you finalize it. Look for a bank that charges no fees for savings accounts.

- **Certificate of Deposit** accounts, called CDs, are different than the more basic savings accounts. When you put money into a CD, you choose a specific amount, say $3,000, and you leave it there until a certain agreed or preset date. During the time your money is in the CD, you'll have to pay a penalty if you want to get the money out early. At the end of the agreed time period, you can withdraw the money without penalty and get paid a higher rate of interest than you would receive from a regular savings account.

The ranges of time that you must leave your money in the CD vary, frequently between six months and five years.

Usually, the longer the term of the CD, the more interest it pays you. If you put money in CDs, research the details beforehand.

Again, you won't need this until you have built up around $5,000 in your regular savings. Once you've reached this milestone (which we are only suggesting as a good rule of thumb), putting part of your money in CDs can make it a better asset (because it pays you more). Talk to your parents before putting any money into CDs. Workers at your bank can help explain the details to you and your parents as needed.

Note that even though CDs pay much more interest than regular savings accounts, they still tend to pay fairly low amounts and are not really a very good deal these days. CDs are really not investments. They are just a way to get a little bit more from your savings.

Before looking at CDs, be sure to study the investment chapters later on in this book. Know all the options before you make big money decisions. This applies to adults as well as teens.

- An **Automatic Savings Plan** can be a very good option if you have a regular job and/or paycheck. An automatic savings plan is where your bank receives your paycheck each month (or every two weeks, for example) and automatically deposits a certain amount (predetermined by you) in your savings and the rest into your checking account for you to spend.

  This simply skips the necessity for you to count up your money, divide it into piles, and send some to savings, some to giving, and some to spending. With such a plan, your bank does parts of this for you.

Obviously, if you have a hard time disciplining yourself to save and give before you spend, this can be very helpful. It doesn't do much good for most youth, however, because your income isn't so regular. It often comes at different times and in differing amounts. This is true of many business owners as well.

But if you are on a set salary or paycheck, such a plan can be very helpful.

In general, we recommend that all adults have a savings account and that teens get a savings account and learn how to use it. This process can help you build up funds and start receiving a bit of interest, however small, over time.

Warnings

Please read the following very carefully. These could really save you a lot of problems in your life. Finance expert Amy Fontinelle suggested the following protections as you use your savings and any other bank accounts:[6]

- In a world with rampant identity theft, it is important to be very careful in how you handle your private information. Don't give out your savings account number, obviously. Don't write your social security number (or equivalent in other nations) or driver's license number on checks that you write—or anywhere else, for that matter. Always be careful with your personal information. This is especially important when you shop online or even just interact online with other people in social media or other ways.

- If you live in the United States, only use banks that are insured by FDIC. This means that they are required to meet and follow all the federal safety issues to protect your money. In Canada the CDIC fulfills the same function. If you live somewhere else, look up your nation's equivalent.

- Don't ever do your banking online in a public place like the library or a business network—even if you're using your own computer. This just makes identity theft** much easier.

- If your bank contacts you with an e-mail and wants any of your personal information, be skeptical. It's probably someone who wants to steal from you. Banks won't send such online requests. Never click any of the links in such an e-mail. If this happens, go to the bank and ask them about it in person.

- The same is true if any people call you and say they are from your bank. Never give any personal information over the phone. Go to the bank in person if needed. This can help you avoid both scams and identity theft.

If you aren't an adult, always discuss with your parents any changes in your accounts or how you want to use them. This is an important part of the learning process. Also, never withdraw from your savings without discussing the reason with your parents. This will help you grow the savings asset, instead of whittling away at it without realizing how quickly it can disappear.

Your savings account with your bank can be a great blessing to you. As you are consistent in depositing your predetermined

---

** See Financial Glossary for definition if you're unfamiliar with this term.

percentage of all money you make, over time, you'll be excited and sometimes amazed at how steadily your savings can grow. For many of you, this is your first major asset, and it will help your life in countless ways.

YOUTH
Call to Action

A. Talk to your parents about the value of a savings account, and open one at the bank you choose together. Put some of the money you have already saved in your account to open it. Keep some of your savings in cash, and keep it in a safe place in your home.

B. Carefully read and discuss the warnings in this chapter with your parents.

C. Put your savings account ledger booklet in your finances box, and always keep it up to date. Include updating it as part of your monthly income statement session. Or if you prefer, keep your savings account updated on a spreadsheet or similar method.

D. Mainly: Keep building your savings by always making your predetermined percentage savings deposit on all money you earn or receive.

PARENTS & OTHER ADULTS
Call to Action

1. If you are a parent, carefully read and discuss the warnings in this chapter with your youth.

2. If you haven't already done it, open a savings account, and begin putting at least 10% of all money you earn into it immediately each time you are paid.

3. In addition to your regular savings account, open another savings account and put your emergency fund savings in it. Build it up to $1,000 and then to $5,000. This will greatly improve your financial fitness.

4. Adopt an asset-building path for life. This is one of the most important decisions you can make for your own future and the future of your family.

"No guts, no glory...."

TOOL #11

Your Checking Accounts and Debit Cards

Buy your paper checks from Costco or Walmart.
You don't have to get them from your financial institution;
we found bargain prices at these two retailers.
—CONSUMER REPORTS

Do It Again

A lot of the details we covered in the last chapter also apply to checking accounts and debit cards as well. As a teen, when you are ready to open a checking account (after discussing it with your parents and determining that it is needed or helpful), go to the bank and set it up.

Take your parents (they'll still have to cosign with you), take some money to deposit into your account as you open it, and talk to the workers at the bank. It's good to have a sense of about how many checks you're planning to use per month—this will help the bank official give you the best recommendations for what kind of account features you want.

It is also helpful to you in deciding if you really need a checking account. If you're going to write less than two checks a month, a checking account may not be all that helpful to you. But if you are building a little business and will have more than two purchases a month, a checking account might really help you. In fact, it will help you keep your records a lot more easily.

How Do They Work?

The most important thing to remember is that in some very important ways a check is just like cash. Meaning: when you spend the amount you write on the check, it's gone out of your account. Your checking account works like this:

- You deposit money into your account.
- You can write a check on money you put into your account.
- When you give the check to a person or business, they'll get the amount of your check out of your account.

It seems pretty simple. But for some reason, a lot of people struggle with checking accounts. For example, there is an old joke about a woman who goes shopping, picks out what she wants to buy in the store, and then takes it to the cashier to pay. When the cashier tells her how much it costs, she writes a check for it. Then she does the same thing at the next store, and the next.

A few days later a letter comes from the bank telling her and her husband that they only had $250 in their checking account, but that her checks at the stores added up to $700—and now the bank and the stores want their money. Of course, the woman's husband asks her why she spent so much.

"I didn't even spend all we have!" she replies, pulling out her checkbook and showing her husband that it still holds many unwritten checks. "See, I still have checks!"

She obviously doesn't understand how checks work. A surprising number of men and women make similar mistakes. It's not how many *checks* you *have*, it's how many dollars you have in the checking account. You should only write a check for money you actually have in your account. And once you give it, that money isn't yours anymore.

Again, this is very basic, and most people understand it. But it is surprising how many people struggle with their checkbooks and checking accounts. If you always keep track of how much you have in your checking account, and don't write checks for money you don't have, you'll be fine.

But this means you have to pay close attention.

Three Options

In fact, you'll want to decide which method of paying for things is best for you and your needs right now. Three main possibilities are cash, a checkbook, and a debit card (which we'll explain in detail in a moment). Or you could use a mixture of two or more of these.

It's okay to use one of these methods now and then shift to another one in a year or two. Most adults end up using all three, but most adults typically use one of them a lot more than the other two.

Let's learn some details as well as the major pros and cons of all three options.

The Cash Approach

The cash approach simply means using cash to pay for everything you buy. Here's how the cash approach works. Every time you make money, divide it into three piles: Save, Give, and the Rest. Sounds familiar, doesn't it? Deposit the Save money immediately into your savings account, and mail or take the Give money to your church or whomever you're donating it to. Then put "the rest" of the money in an envelope and use it as needed. But carefully—once you run out, you run out.

You can even get more detailed. Have five or six envelopes, and break "the rest" of the money up the way you plan to use it. For example, on one envelope write "lemonade stand supplies," on another write "monthly phone costs," and on another write "extra." Then be disciplined and only spend money on what it's really for.

You might add an envelope labeled "Disney World Trip" and keep adding to it month after month to save for a big event. (This is what we called "Targeted Savings" earlier in the book.) You can use the envelopes for whatever you want, and use as many as you need.

As the adults learned earlier, the cash method can be a very effective way to budget and manage all your money.

This cash approach is much easier than managing a checking account, and it can help you prepare for effectively using a checking account when the time comes. As you get older, a checking account will eventually be necessary.

Teens need to learn to use checks and keep their checking accounts straight at some point, so don't wait forever. But don't just pick checks when the cash approach really does work much better for you. Talk to your parents about what is best for you right now.

Some adults learn that they're always more effective using the cash method. If that applies to you, do what works.

The Checkbook Approach

As a young person, you don't have to use a checkbook until you're ready. When you do decide to use a checking account, you need to really manage it well. This is very important. And it takes some effort.

Here are the four simple steps of properly taking care of a checking account:

1. Deposit money into your account. When you get paid or receive a gift of money, simply put it into the checking account. You can do this with both checks and cash in person at the bank, and you can get apps that let you deposit a check by smartphone directly to your account.

2. When you want to spend money from your checking account, you can either go to the bank and withdraw the cash you need, or you can write a check for it. When you write a check, you need to make sure that you also write down the check number, who it was written to, and how much it was written for. Write these all down in the check register booklet that comes with your checks when you buy them.

    Make sure you only write checks for money you actually have in your checking account.

3. Every month the bank will send you an account statement for your checking account. Carefully go through it, and compare it to what you wrote in your check register. Record any fees the bank charged you in your register.

141

4. Reconcile the ledger with the bank statement. This means making sure that the statement has the very same entries and the very same total for how much you still have in your checking account as you do in your ledger.

    Have your parents help you with this step the first few months until you get the hang of things. It's not that difficult, but if you make a mistake while doing this (or write out a check for money you don't actually have in your account) the bank can charge you expensive fees.

    Again: Make sure you do all four of these steps. Have your parents help you until you know how to do this, and after that be careful to do steps three and four every month.

It may be helpful to get overdraft protection on your checking account (discuss it with your parents and your bank), which means that the bank will pay the checks you write even if they go above the amount in your account (as long as it's not too much). But they'll charge you big fees for every check when this happens. Again, paying such fees is too expensive for anyone who wants to be financially fit. It's just throwing away money.

The right way is to take charge of your checking account and always update it to know how much money you actually have. This may all sound difficult or complex, but it really isn't. If you follow the four steps consistently, it will be very easy for you.

The Debit Card Approach

Another option is a debit card. These cards look like credit cards, but they act like checks. When you pay for something with a debit card, the money comes directly out of your checking account, the way it would if you wrote a check instead. The main difference is that the charge usually posts immediately, so your online banking will show you a more up-to-date picture of your account.

For this reason, many parents prefer to teach their youth the cash method, followed by learning to use a debit card, and only later a checking account. In essence, a debit card purchase is just another sort of check. In fact, as Amy Fontinelle put it, debit cards are "sometimes called…check card[s]."[7]

Some debit cards can also be used to withdraw cash from an automated teller machine (ATM). To use them this way, you'll receive a personal identification number (PIN) from the bank, and you'll have to know it by memory and use it to access your account on any ATM. It usually costs you a fee to withdraw cash from an ATM, however. In an emergency, it is helpful. In most other situations, it's just a waste of money.

Again, those who learn these skills will understand all types of financial accounts more easily and deeply.

Note that most debit cards are attached to a checking account, so if you're going to write checks and also use the card, you need to do everything we outlined above with a checking account. Alternatively, you can skip the checks and only use the debit card.

For adults: Debit cards can also be much better than credit cards if you have trouble with overspending and need a credit card to fly, rent a car, buy airfare, check into a hotel, or make other business payments.

Prepaid Credit Cards

Some people prefer something called prepaid credit cards, because they can use cash to get the card and then keep track of spending easily online. If this works for you, great. It's a variation of the cash approach.

But many prepaid cards have a lot of hidden extra fees. For example, *Consumer Reports* warned: "If you decide that a prepaid card is a more convenient way to manage your spending money, shop carefully. Some charge fees for reloading or withdrawing money, or for just making a balance inquiry, among other drawbacks."[8] Many prepaid cards also charge very high overdraft fees.[9]

Three things to look for: (1) all the fees and costs of using the card, (2) whether or not your account is always up to date and available online (without extra fees), and (3) whether or not your account will do everything a checking account will do.

Note that you can usually only buy prepaid cards in a store like Walmart and some grocery stores+ and that they aren't protected the way debit cards connected to your bank account are.[10] Overall, they might be useful for specific purposes, but they aren't the best substitute for one of the other methods.

Summary

The cash and envelope method outlined above is probably best for most teens, at least to start. And a lot of adults use it to really get ahold of their finances.

But it is also important to start learning to use checking accounts while you are young. One of the best ways to learn the needed skills is to follow the four step process described above, and then scale up with monthly entry of receipts into your spreadsheet. Again, those who learn these skills will understand all types of financial accounts more easily and deeply.

At some point a checking account will be very helpful, provided you manage it consistently and carefully. It's certainly best to try to learn this while your finances are simple rather than waiting until they are a lot more complex.

YOUTH
Call to Action

A. With your parents, discuss the three methods of handling your money outlined in this chapter: cash, checking account, and debit card. Which makes most sense for you and your needs right now in your life? If you're not sure, start with cash. Or if safety is a concern, discuss a debit card.

B. Whichever method you use, spend some time and effort to learn how to do it right. Don't be lax on this. If you're ready to use a checking account, for example, or want to learn, manage it carefully as outlined above. Get your parents' help each time you reconcile your checkbook—at least for the first few months. Note that some people use the term "balance your checkbook" rather than "reconcile your checkbook."

C. Ask your parents whatever questions come up as you are learning how to do this.

PARENTS & OTHER ADULTS
Call to Action

1. Do you ever end up paying extra bank fees on any of your accounts or cards? If so, avoid extra fees by keeping a close watch on all your accounts. Get better at this by putting some real effort into it right now. Make it a project! It will immediately save you money.

2. Which do you use most: the cash, checkbooks, or debit card option? Or do you use the fourth option: credit cards? (See the next chapter.) Take some time to consider which would truly be best for you right now. If you ever have a hard time with overspending or overdrafts, making ends meet or conquering debt, seriously look at the benefits of the cash method. It's not just for teens; it's excellent for adults as well.

"Nothing succeeds like success...."

Credit Cards—To Be or Not to Be...

*To not understand the language of money today
is to be an economic slave.*
—JOHN HOPE BRYANT

*If you have no debt and $10 in your pocket,
you are better off financially
than 25 percent of Americans.*
—CREDIT SUISSE

The Chainsaw Principle

Chainsaws are very dangerous tools. If you need to cut a lot of firewood down to size, they are often the best tool for the job. But if you don't know what you are doing, you're probably going to get hurt. And when you get hurt by a chainsaw, it's a major disaster. Therefore, if you don't know how to handle a chainsaw, you probably shouldn't even pick one up.

The same could be said of cars, trucks and other motor vehicles. They are great for many kinds of transportation, but if a driver doesn't know what he's doing, he's in real trouble—and so are all the people near him as he drives down the road. If you don't know how to handle a car, you probably shouldn't even climb into the driver's seat.

This principle—call it the Chainsaw Principle—applies to a number of items, from firearms to motorboats to fireworks and beyond. Some are wonderful tools in the right hands but still very dangerous. And usually such things are best left entirely alone by those who don't know what they're doing.

Guess what? Credit cards might just be at the very top of the list when it comes to these kinds of risks. More people have done more damage to themselves and their families with credit cards than anything else we can think of. Millions of people have glee-fully taken a credit card in hand and caused themselves massive harm, even years of frustration and pain, sometimes in the space of just a few hours or days.

Credit cards are financially dangerous.

They are also, like cars and boats and chainsaws, very effective tools—in the right hands. Use them the right way, and they can be a great blessing to your financial life. But use them the wrong way, even a little, and your financial fitness can take a major hit.

What Are Credit Cards?

Credit cards were originally created to make spending money easier—but this is a two-edged sword. If you find it so easy that you don't stay disciplined, you can cause real problems for your finances.

Before credit cards were developed, as we explained in the previous chapter, people had to use cash or a check every time they made a purchase. For example, consider a person who travels to a distant town to do business for a week or more and eats all his meals at the town diner. He might find it frustrating to have to pay for each breakfast, lunch, and dinner separately.

To make this more convenient, some restaurants began offering a "diner's card," which allowed the consumer to charge a number of meals at one restaurant—and then pay for it all with one bill at the end of the week or month. The idea caught on, and companies began offering cards that were accepted by many stores—not just restaurants.

To make it financially viable, they either charged a fee for the card and fees for each transaction, or they charged interest if people ran up a lot of expenses on a card and then didn't pay it off each month. Today, many people have credit cards—which combine most or even all of their monthly expenses and then give them one convenient bill at a specific time during the month.

The problem for some people is that this became *too* convenient. It is so easy to charge things to a card without really noticing how much you are spending. Many people spend more than they have, without even realizing it. They frequently buy things they don't really need or even want very much, because it's just so easy and painless to whip out a credit card to pay for them.

> **Whether or not you should use a credit card as a financial tool in your life is largely a matter of your "financial temperament."**

What happens is that these purchases quickly add up. At the end of the month when the credit card bill comes, people discover that they've spent a lot more than they intended. If they don't have enough money (in their savings or checking account) to pay the credit card bill (by sending the credit card company enough money to pay them back for covering the purchases all month long), then a "balance" results on the credit card. At this point, the credit card company starts charging interest on the unpaid balance. These interest rates are generally pretty high.

As a result, today many people pay a lot of their monthly income to credit card expenses and interest. This is a serious problem for their financial fitness.

Temperament

Whether or not you should use a credit card as a financial tool in your life is largely a matter of your "financial temperament." What does this mean? Your temperament is simply the way you choose to deal with things.

When we're talking about finances, we don't mean the kind of temperament often compared in personality style books—like "fiery," "calm," "melancholy," "always laughing," "plodding," or "plotting." We mean something very different. And it's very important.

Moreover, it's not part of your personality style at all. It can be learned, and those who are financially successful have learned to do it right—to always maintain the right financial temperament. Especially when it comes to credit cards.

The right financial temperament is that of learning the principles, following the principles, not deviating from the principles, and sticking with the right principles no matter what.

Now, that might sound like a certain personality type to you, but it isn't. People from all personality types have learned to adopt the right temperament. It's not a matter of style; it's a matter of choice.

Those who want to be financially fit and financially successful have learned that there are certain financial principles that you can't break if you want to succeed. And so they always follow these principles.

They earn, and they do it before they spend. Always. They never break this rule. They know that breaking it puts them on a path to financial problems.

> Those who want to be financially fit and financially successful have learned that there are certain financial principles that you can't break if you want to succeed. And so they always follow these principles.

Since they'd rather be on a path to financial success, they simply never stop saving. They save every time they get money. Always. No exceptions. Without fail.

This isn't a personality type; it's a decision. And financially successful people follow it.

Likewise, people who want to be financially fit know that the only way to get there is to delay gratification. So they do it. There are many other examples—including a lot of the tools outlined in this book.

> When leaders see that a certain principle or behavior is necessary for real success, they follow it.

Again, people who do these things consistently develop a certain "financial temperament." In their everyday life they might be silly or stern. They might naturally be brooding or always contemplating things. They might be deep thinkers, skeptics, or social butterflies who always seem happy and fun. They might be melancholy or sanguine, introverted or extroverted. They might be any of the personality types covered in all the books and apps on personality types.

But when it comes to leadership, they have a similar temperament. When they see that a certain principle or behavior is necessary for real success, they follow it. They make themselves do it. They choose it. And they keep choosing it.

This is the temperament of leadership, and it is the temperament of great financial improvement. Those who follow the principles and tools improve. Those who don't...don't. It's that simple.

How to Have the Right Temperament

When it comes to credit cards, people with the right financial temperament always (always!) do the following:

- Pay the credit card bill off in full every month (and therefore don't pay any interest or late fees).

Do this, and credit cards can be a very helpful tool for you. Otherwise, stick with a debit card, checks, or cash.

Now, knowing that they will pay the full card off every month, such people are also very careful to never spend money they don't already have. They never buy something on a credit card (or any other way) unless they already have the money.

They never say, "Well, three weeks from now I'll have the money, so I guess it's okay to buy this now. After all, this is such a good sale. It might not be repeated."

Instead, they say: "I'll come back in three weeks when I have the money. If I can still get a good deal, great. If not, I may or may not buy it. But I never buy anything unless I have the money already."

This is the right temperament.

People who follow these principles are on the path to financial success. Those who don't follow the principles usually live lives of financial struggle.

The Credit Card Rules

That's the first rule of credit cards. The first two rules, actually:

1. Pay off every credit card (the whole balance in full) every month, paying no interest or fees.
2. Never buy anything with a credit card unless you already have the money.

Here are some other important rules:

3. Carefully study every credit card statement when it arrives, and make sure all the charges are legitimate (a lot of people steal credit card numbers and use them—so make sure every bill only contains things you actually bought).
4. Be careful where you use your cards (e.g., don't use insecure sites online, or public computers) to guard your privacy.
5. Make sure to always, always, always follow rules 1 and 2.

People who follow these rules carefully and consistently have the right temperament to use credit cards. People who don't unswervingly follow these rules don't have the right temperament and shouldn't use credit cards.

Practicalities

As for youth using credit cards, it's up to parents to decide what to do. One thing is certain: if the parents don't have the right temperament (if they don't follow all five rules all the time), they shouldn't dole out a credit card to their teen. This is true even if the teen does have the right temperament.

Why? Because parents are ultimately responsible for the minor's card and any charges on it. Parents with the wrong temperament are going to have a serious problem with any credit card—they'll frequently pay huge amounts of wasted money to interest and possibly late fees.

It's just not a good fit to have credit cards in a home where the parents have the wrong temperament for credit cards. When the teen grows up, she can make her own decisions.

But what if the parents do have the right temperament and do consistently follow the rules of good credit card use? Such parents can do their teen a lot of good by helping her learn to use a credit card the right way. Meaning: follow all five rules, always.

> People who follow these principles are on the path to financial success. Those who don't follow the principles usually live lives of financial struggle.

The question is simply: Is *now* the right time for this youth to learn these lessons? If so, do it. If not, hold off. The right time will come.

The real needs of the youth are to (1) have some way to pay for things, both business and personal, and (2) learn how to effectively use the right money tools for financial fitness. The first of these items combines what we've learned in this chapter and the last chapter. What is the best way for Jenny or Bobby or Carol to spend and manage his or her money right now and for the next year or so? Is it the cash option, a debit card, a checking account, or a credit card? (Or some mixture of these?)

Clearly, item (2) above tells us that Jenny will learn the most by understanding all of these methods and having experiences with each. But that doesn't mean that *right now* is the time to use all the methods. It's almost always best to learn one of these methods at a time, and the cash method should usually come first. (As mentioned, in some locales parents opt for debit cards for safety reasons.)

Parents should seriously consider what is the best option right now for each youth—and adopt that option. Others can be added later, when the parents feel it is right.

Indeed, adults need to make this same decision for themselves. If you are deeply in debt and trying to get a real handle on your spending, for example, the cash option is likely the best for you right now. The credit card option is definitely not a good idea.

Consider all four options, and choose the best for you at this point in your life.

Warnings and Recommendations

As we said above, if you need a card for travel, hotels, flights, work, etc., but your past history suggests that you'll struggle to follow the credit card rules, get a debit card instead. And only use it for these purchases.

If you struggle with credit cards but have some in your home or wallet, cut them up. Or if you might need them for emergencies, fill a bucket with water and freeze it with the credit card in the middle. If you ever need it for real, you'll have to wait for the ice to melt or get out a hammer and dig it out.

Either way, you'll have to really work for it. This slows down the time between when you first feel the desire to buy that cool new drone you just saw on a late-night television infomercial and when you can actually make the call and spend the money.

It gives you more time to come to your senses and for your spouse to hear you pounding ice in the kitchen and come down-stairs to find out who's remodeling the house. All of these are good roadblocks to a bad decision. But ultimately, it's going to come down to you deciding. Debt or Asset? It's up to you.

YOUTH
Call to Action

Closely study the five credit card rules listed in this chapter. Can you follow them exactly, consistently? Choose now to develop this discipline, and begin putting it into action, even before you have a credit card.

PARENTS AND OTHER ADULTS
Call to Action

1. Closely study the five credit card rules in this chapter. If you use a credit card, begin applying these rules for all credit card purchases from now on, if you aren't already doing so. Simultaneously begin paying down your current credit card balance(s), if any, by paying extra to your card with the lowest balance and highest interest rate every time you get paid. Do this consistently. When one card balance is paid off, keep doing this with the next lowest balance—and repeat.

2. Seriously consider which of the four methods discussed in this and the last chapter is best for you right now in your life. Decide upon one and follow it consistently.

"A penny saved is a penny earned...."

Snakes in the Grass:
So Many Hidden Costs

*The most important quality
for an investor is temperament, not intellect.*
—WARREN BUFFETT

So Many of Them!

There are a lot of hidden costs in the modern world. In fact, we could write a whole book just about these sneaky expenses. Then we'd give it a really cool title:

*Snakes in the Grass:
So Many Snakes in the Grass*

Okay, that's weird. Maybe, instead, we'd name the book:

The Hunger Games—Part 7: Hidden Costs

Or not. Maybe we'd better not write the book at all, since we can't come up with a good title for it. It's just not meant to be, apparently. But we are going to cover the main hidden costs in this chapter anyway. Knowing them and making them part of your financial decision-making is extremely important.

Let's start with one of the biggest hidden costs of all, taxes.

Since the First Governments

Taxes have been around for a long time. In fact, there's an old saying that the only things that are certain in life are death and taxes. That's a pretty intense list of two. But taxes have been with us as long as governments, even the earliest, most informal governments.

In modern times, governments are sure to get their cut of everyone's money. They do this in three ways: (1) taxation, (2) regulation, and (3) tampering with the money supply. What does this all mean? Let's walk through it step by step.

So you're a teen and you want to buy a car or pay for new clothes or get your books for a college class—or, in a few years once you're married, buy a house for your family to live in.

Well, first, whatever money you earn, the government wants a piece of it. This means that when you're saving your 50 percent of all income, at the end of the year the government is going to come and want part of it. Most teens don't make enough money in a year that they owe very much, if any, but if they do, the government wants it.

Or if you make money at an evening or weekend job at the burger joint or the local grocery mart, the government will take a chunk of each of your paychecks before you even get paid. If you make $8 an hour, for example, and you work for 20 hours this week, you're expecting to get paid $160. But the government will take some of your money, so when you get your check for something like $134.40, you think there's been a huge mistake.

When you ask your employer about it, however, you find out that the additional money went to taxes. The first time this happens, a lot of young people walk around in shock for a while. (Many adults do the same thing over and over every year when they find out how much their taxes will cost—or each time they get their paycheck and see how much was withheld.)

But the government doesn't just take money out for taxes. It also takes out additional money for things called Social Security, Medicare, etc. In every country, the government has its own names for these taxes and other fees that are treated like taxes.

> **Knowing the hidden costs and making them part of your financial decision-making is extremely important.**

So that's the first step. You want to buy your first car or your books for a college class or something else, but before you even head to the car dealer, the government has already taxed the money you earned.

More Taxes by Other Names

The next step occurs when you go with your parents to a car dealer or to someone selling a car in the local newspaper and make a really good deal on your first little used car. You negotiate the price down to something you can barely afford, even though you've been saving especially for this day (beyond your normal 50 percent savings) for a long time.

Then you pull out your checkbook (or cash or debit card if the seller accepts debit cards), and the seller tells you a price way higher than the one you just agreed to.

"What?" you ask in astonishment.

"It's okay," your parents tell you. "He just added tax, registration, and environmental fees."

"Huh?"

"It's normal."

But it doesn't feel very normal to you. You look to make sure you have the extra money, and if you don't, you stop right there and say, "I don't have that much extra money. I'll have to come back when I do."

And you walk away. You have the right financial temperament. Awesome!

If you *do* have the money, and if you decide the car is worth it even at the higher price caused by all these unexpected hidden costs, you take a deep breath and write the check. If you're unsure, say so. "I'm not ready right now. I need to sleep on this."

Never buy when your gut isn't sure. Seriously. Wait.

Once you're sure and you've made the purchase, you walk outside with your parents and you ask: "Taxes, registration, and environmental fee? What's up with all that?"

They tell you that what you may not realize yet is that the government also has regulations, beyond all these taxes (and various things called "fees" that are actually just more taxes).

"Wait, regulations?" you ask. "What does that mean to me right now?"

It means that before you can start using your new little used car, you're going to have to pay insurance on it. Why? Because the government requires it. The government regulated it, meaning that they made a rule that you have to do it. That's a regulation.

And guess what, after all the taxes are already taken from your paycheck, you've already paid the taxes and registration and fees to get your car, and you've already paid for the government-required insurance, you'll want to drive your car around. You'll go to the gas station to put some fuel in your car, and you'll see that you have to pay a huge tax on every gallon or liter of gas you put in your tank.

At some point, the young person learning all this begins to wonder. Seriously?

The answer is yes. There are hidden costs. Taxes and regulation cause a lot of them. And while governments are important for matters like national security and law enforcement, there's no doubt that most governments take the levels of taxes and regulations too far.

But you're going to need to pay these costs—if you want to have and drive a car. So when you are saving up for the car, be sure to add the taxes, registration, fees, insurance, and other hidden costs to your savings goals.

If you eventually buy a house, you'll deal with a bunch of similar hidden costs. This is true of almost every major purchase. There are hidden costs on little purchases as well, but most people are used to them. You pay tax on almost anything you buy.

But when it comes to a car or a house, the numbers can feel really high. The solution? First, be entrepreneurial, and earn more money than just the bare minimum. To actually make purchases, you'll need more than you might expect. Second, start studying freedom, and when you're a voter, help move your nation in a better direction because you really understand how governments are supposed to work.

Changing government taxation and regulation is a long-term need. And you can help make a real difference in the world. This is important.

Loans

But there is also something more immediate that you need to know about. When you buy things using a loan, you pay even more hidden costs. And while you probably can't do much about the hidden costs of taxes and regulations right now, you can do a great deal about the hidden costs associated with borrowing. The less you borrow, the fewer such costs you pay.

> A lot of people really ruin their finances because they put status before assets. They care more about what people will think of them than whether or not they're making wise financial decisions.

Consider our two examples: buying a car and buying a home. These may be far in the future for you, or they may be just ahead, but learning about them now can make a big positive difference in your life.

When you buy a car or a home, many of the same principles apply. For example, you've got to put assets above status! This is a big, big deal. A lot of people really ruin their finances because they put atatus before assets. They care more about what people will think of them than whether or not they're making wise financial decisions and building assets rather than just increasing debt.

Don't make this mistake. Don't buy cars for status. And don't buy houses for status. Both of these problems are widespread among Americans, Canadians, and others, and very often just these two bad choices—to buy cars for status, and to buy homes for status—keep people from ever getting ahead financially. Millions of people spend their whole lives financially struggling because they buy cars or homes with status in mind. This poor decision leads to other poor decisions, such as getting loans (with interest and fees) to buy something they really can't afford.

Just don't do this. There is a much better way.

The most ironic thing about all this is that people who buy cars and homes as assets usually build assets over several decades, and then they end up with much bigger and amazing homes than the people who were aiming for status and used loans to buy things. In other words, those who delay their gratification in the short term in order to follow correct financial principles end up with much more in the long run. It's the tortoise beating the hare.

Jon and Carly

A brother and sister, Jon and Carly, had similar goals when they were teens. They both wanted to make a positive difference in the world, to raise a family, to be financially prosperous, and be able to buy the good things in life. They grew up in a poor neighborhood, and both vowed that they'd do things differently as adults.

They were both married by the time they were thirty, and they each built a business with their spouse. Carly and her husband built a large bed and bath shop in the state's biggest city, and they were soon bringing in significant profits beyond their business costs.

Jon and his wife moved several hours away to another part of the state, and he built up an air conditioning business that installed the heating and air ducts in new houses and business buildings. While Jon's business grew more slowly, it was steady, and every few years he expanded.

But there was a major difference in the way they approached their personal expenses. As Carly's business boomed, she and her husband decided that it was a priority to live in the "best" neighborhood, send their kids the most prestigious schools, and be seen as successful by everyone in their community.

They purchased the biggest house the bank said they could afford, with a huge monthly payment on the loan that ate away at much of their business profit, and they spent a lot of money on the most popular decorator in the city. They filled their home with cutting edge brands of furniture, art, and other décor, and they filled their four-car garage with the kinds of vehicles they knew would be the envy of their friends.

They soon found themselves caught in a status trap: to show so much status, they made lots of bad financial choices. Most of this was accomplished with debt, as much as they could get with the strong profits coming from their growing business. They frequently entertained people from the neighborhood and the other "best" parts of the city, and they purposely kept actively involved in the social scene of the city's elite.

Jon and his wife took a different direction. He struggled for several years to get his business established, but as it grew, he looked for opportunities to build relationships with top contractors in the area and bid on bigger contracts. When the business began to flourish, he carefully saved the extra profits and watched for a bigger warehouse.

Two years later he purchased a building that tripled his company's capacity, and he had the cash to hire and buy the machinery to fill the warehouse in a few months. He emphasized leadership and the highest quality in his standards of duct installation, and his company's reputation grew.

During the same time period, Jon and his wife left their two-bedroom rental home and purchased a modest older three-bedroom family home with a nice yard in the part of the town known as "the families and trees section." He upped his personal salary a bit to help pay for the growing children's needs, and he poured most of the company's profits back into building the business.

Ten Years Later

You already know how this turns out, don't you? When an opportunity came for Jon to open two more warehouses in neighboring cities, he had the cash savings, business assets, contracts, and relationships to make it happen. Within a few years he built his family a dream home on twenty-five acres and paid for it all in cash.

When a major construction recession developed in the nation, much of Carly's income at the store dried up, and the couple didn't have the funds to keep paying for their lifestyle. They eventually downgraded, and Carly had to go back to work.

In contrast, Jon and his team were able to shift from local sales to projects in various markets around the nation where the construction economy was still strong. His business actually had to build a fourth warehouse to meet the increased demand.

The Asset Path

During these years, both Jon and Carly used loans at times. But they didn't use them in the same way. Jon paid cash for used cars, and ignored status. Carly used credit to buy expensive cars, trying to boost her status in her own eyes and those of her neighbors.

> **Whenever you use a loan to buy things, you're signing up to pay a lot of hidden costs.**

Jon carefully used a loan to buy his first home—but it was just adequate to his family's needs and he paid extra to the mortgage every month.

At the same time that Carly lost her huge home and had to start renting an apartment, Jon and his wife were living in their dream home—with no mortgage. Carly used debt to start her business and then drained the profits to fund her lifestyle. Jon started small and built only when he had the cash to expand, always trying to avoid debt. When profits came, he put them back into expanding the company.

In short, Carly used debt to fund what she considered to be the needs of status and ended up with few assets. Jon avoided debt as much as he could and focused on building assets—more and more all the time.

> **In the end, the one who built assets had all the status, even though this wasn't his purpose.**

In the end, the one who built assets had all the status, even though this wasn't his purpose. And the one who went after status was left with none—and with huge debts. Seeking status is a waste of your life, and it leaves you short in the end, anyway. To be financially fit, build assets.

Indeed, when Jon used debt, he used it as an asset—to build more assets. Carly tried to use debt like an ATM, and her lifestyle eventually caved in.

The Hidden Costs of Debt

Whenever you use a loan to buy things, you're signing up to pay not only interest, but a lot of hidden costs, including various fees, taxes, etc. Of course, the main hidden cost of any loan is the interest.

Interest is a big deal. Much of the time it's even bigger than taxes.

There are two major kinds of interest: simple interest and compound interest. Simple interest occurs where you agree to a loan for a specific price, such as a $100 loan for 5% interest, payable in three months. Since 5% of $100 is $5, that's the interest you'll pay. This means that in three months you'll owe the lender $105. See, it's simple. But this kind of interest is unusual. Compound interest is the common type of interest.

To demonstrate how "compounding" works, consider the following:

Would you rather receive $100 right now, or a penny today, and then double the amount each day for 30 days? Many people quickly choose the $100, but that's because they don't understand compounding. If the amount you receive is compounded by double every day, the penny quickly increases. A lot.

Day 1: 1 penny
Day 2: 2 pennies
Day 3: 4 pennies
Day 4: 8 pennies
Day 5: 16 pennies
Day 6: 32 pennies

At this point, the person is probably thinking, "I should have taken the $100!"

Day 7: 64 pennies
Day 8: $1.28
Day 9: $2.56
Day 10: $5.12
Day 11: $10.24
Day 12: $20.48
Day 13: $40.96

By now the person is realizing that the $100 was a bad choice.

Day 14: $81.92
Day 15: $163.84

"The $100 would have been a very, very bad choice," the person is telling himself. "I'm only half way to the thirty days, and I'll get more than $100 a day every day from now on!"

Day 16: $327.68
Day 17: $655.36
Day 18: $1,310.72
Day 19: $2,621.44
Day 20: $5,242.88

Right about now the person is shocked by the power of compounding.

Day 21: $10,485.76
Day 22: $20,971.52
Day 23: $41,943.04
Day 24: $83,886.08
Day 25: $167,772.16

As you can now see, compounding is amazing! Understanding it is essential if you want to be financially fit.

Day 26: $335,544.32
Day 27: $671,088.64
Day 28: $1,342,177.28
Day 29: $2,684,354.56
Day 30: $5,368,709.12

So, again, would you prefer $100 on day 1, or over $5 million on day 30? Take the compounding! Unless this is a debt you owe, in which case take the $100.

Oh, and by the way, the way compounding works is you add up the entire amount the person received each of the thirty days and it comes to $10,737,089.91.

As the above example clearly shows, compound interest is very different than simple interest. It also charges a set rate, like 5%, but it calculates and adds to it repetitively. For example, if you got a $100 loan at 5% interest compounded daily, you'd owe $105 the next day, $110.25 the second day, $115.76 the third day, $121.55 the fourth day, $127.63 the fifth day, $134.01 the sixth day, and $140.71 the seventh day.

Now that's some serious interest! Within a week you've accrued nearly half of what you borrowed just in interest. Keep this going and you'll be paying thousands or tens of thousands of dollars for a $100 loan. When you hear "old" people lecturing about the evils of interest, you can see what they're so upset about. That's why Albert Einstein said that compound interest is the eighth wonder of the world!

Of course, banks that loan you money for a car purchase or home mortgage don't compound the interest in this extreme manner, but any compounding quickly and drastically raises your price. For example, if you have $5,000 on your credit card and you only make the minimum payment each month, depending on the interest rate, it will take you approximately 26–29 years to pay it off, and the total amount you'll pay, including interest, ranges between $11,000 and more than $14,000!

And it's not uncommon for interest rates to be much higher than this. Compound interest costs—a lot!

Mortgages

A mortgage is a debt you owe on your house, and most mortgages are set up to be paid back over a thirty-year period. Just consider how much compounding increases when you buy a house. Many people end up paying around triple what they thought the house would cost them—because of the hidden costs of compound interest. Orrin Woodward strongly recommends that people follow the 2X Rule: Don't buy a home that costs more than two times what you make annually. In this way you will be able to afford larger payments than the minimum and thereby pay off the loan way early, dodging tens of thousands of dollars in interest costs.

Banks frequently suggest that you can spend a lot more than that on a home, but they are the ones who charge you compound interest on it. The 2X Rule is a much better plan.

Saving up the money to make a big down payment on your home purchase will save you a lot of money in the long run. In fact, there are two main kinds of mortgages: (1) those with very small down payments and higher monthly payments, and (2) those with larger down payments and smaller monthly payments.

The second is much better. Save for a down payment, and make it as big as you can. It will pay you back a lot over the years by way of less interest.

Save for a down payment, and make it as big as you can. It will pay you back a lot over the years by way of less interest.

Moreover, when it comes to buying a home, Chris Brady reminds us that renting is often the better approach—until you've saved at least a significant part of the cost in cash for the home you purchase. Renting might also be a good idea if houses are going down in value, allowing you to wait and get a better deal on one later while at the same time allowing you more time to save up a bigger down payment.

Insurance Can Help

There is one hidden cost that is often a big blessing—insurance. In fact, if you ever need insurance, it's a great asset. But always remember that the cost of insurance should be figured into any purchase that requires it. We'll say more about insurance in a later chapter. But never leave insurance out of any consideration of "big ticket" items you're considering buying.

Summary

Hopefully, after reading about all these hidden costs, you can see why we thought about naming a book on this topic:

Snakes in the Grass:
So Many Snakes in the Grass

or

The Hunger Games—Part 7: Hidden Costs

They really do fit. But seriously, when you make financial plans, don't forget to factor in the hidden costs. To summarize, some of the major hidden costs to always look for include (but aren't limited to):

- Taxes
- Registrations, licenses, fees, and other "taxes by other names"
- Regulations
- Insurance
- Interest

YOUTH
Call to Action

A. Make sure you understand the things covered in this chapter. In places this chapter was a bit deeper than some of the earlier chapters, but the material here is extremely important.

B. Discuss the key points in this chapter with your parents. For example:

- Why should we always put assets before status?
- Define "compound interest." Why is it such a big deal?
- What is the best way to prepare for a mortgage?
- What is the 2X Rule? Why is it so important?
- What is the difference between the asset path and the debt path? Which are you on right now? Which do you want to be on? Why?

PARENTS AND OTHER ADULTS
Call to Action

Complete Exercise B in the Youth section above with your teens and young adults. Or if you don't have children this age, find someone to discuss these points with you. Talking about them will help you remember and apply them. Read the chapter together, and talk about these questions. They are very important.

"Compound interest is the eighth wonder of the world...."

PART THREE

THINK LIKE THE BEST
INVESTORS AND LEADERS

"Strike while the iron is hot...."

TOOL #14

A Major Secret!

"Don't be in a hurry to get more things.
Focus instead on becoming a better leader
and financial decision maker
and on having more real resources."
—CHRIS BRADY

Did You Know?

Let's discuss another major hidden cost that most people don't know about. In fact, this is really more of a "hidden benefit." It only costs you if you don't know about it and don't use it.

We've already addressed this a little bit in earlier chapters, but it deserves more attention now that we're talking about hidden costs. This hidden expense is a huge secret to many teens and adults alike, and it quietly makes the difference between financial fitness and financial failure for a lot of people. And for others, it makes things a lot harder, even though they work and achieve financial fitness anyway.

We're talking about the fact that for people on the job or career path of making their living, most of the hidden costs outlined in this chapter have to be paid out of their personal money. But for business owners, a lot of these hidden costs can be paid for by the business. This is because the government allows business owners to deduct from taxable income certain expenses that people who earn paychecks from a job cannot. This deduction lowers the amount of taxes a business owner has to pay. It's a big advantage.

This difference being able to do this makes can have a huge impact on one's finances. Let's compare the choices of two fictional people to see how this works:

Billy and Liz

Billy makes his living at a job or salaried career, while Liz makes her living as a business owner. Both of them decide they need another car to get their work done well, and they research and purchase a good, solid, used, still beautiful Buick. (Okay, the Buick might not be very cool, but hopefully it's reliable. Billy will be sad if you call it his granny car.)

Both of them negotiate with the dealer to buy their car for $12,000, and both of them pay in cash.

Here's the hidden cost for Billy. He has to pay for the car with after-tax income. This means that to earn the $12,000 for the car, he needs to earn enough money that the government can take its cut out of his paychecks and he'll still have $12,000 left over.

In other words, Billy ends up making something close to $13,884 in order to pay the taxes and also the $12,000 for the car. Then he has to pay the additional taxes, registration, and fees for the car, something like $1,160 (depending on what nation, province, or state he lives in and what their exact requirements are). But again, to get the $1,160, he needs to earn enough at work that the government can take its cut from his paycheck and he'll still have the $1,160 left over. The actual amount is something more like $1,342.

It adds up quickly, doesn't it? That's how hidden costs work. Now, before he brings the car to his driveway, Billy needs to buy insurance for it. He shops around and gets a rate he's comfortable with, with more than the bare minimum of coverage, at $735 every six months (or $1,470 a year). But this money also comes after taxes. The amount he had to earn in order to pay taxes and have this left over is around $1700.

Because of hidden costs, Billy's total for this car is $16,927 rather than the basic $12,000 he negotiated with the dealer. Still, he's got his car. Cool. It will really help him in his job or career.

BILLY	
Car Purchase	12,000
Taxes, regulations, fees	1,160
Insurance	1,470
Total	$14,630
What Billy had to earn to pay for this	$16,927

Another Path

Liz buys the same model and make of car in the same county on the same day. But since the car is needed for her company, she has her business buy it. The business doesn't have to take taxes out before the purchase, so the total cost including taxes, registration, fees and insurance is $14,630.

LIZ	
Car Purchase	12,000
Taxes, regulations, fees	1,160
Insurance	1,470
Total	$14,630
What her company had to earn in order to pay for this	$14,630

"But wait," you say. "Why does Liz get to pay $2,300 less than Billy? For the same car! That's not fair."

This is a major advantage given to business owners. For Liz the car is a before-taxes business expense. For Billy, it's a personal purchase. The difference in what they have to pay is the result of the favorable tax situation given to businesses so they can prosper.

Amazingly, there's more. Again, this is all about hidden costs. Let's say in the next month both Billy and Liz earn a major bonus. Billy's job bonus pays him $20,000, and Liz's business gets paid a $20,000 bonus for her work as well. Pretty great, right?

What are the hidden costs on this bonus? Well, when Billy gets his bonus check from his employer it's going to be around $16,860. Why is it smaller than $20,000? By now you already understand this. Because of the taxes, Social Security, and Medicare that are withheld from it before Billy even gets it.

Liz, on the other hand, will get a check for her business in the amount of $20,000. Of course, her business has to pay taxes too, but they're structured differently. Liz will take the $20,000 of income from the bonus and put that on her business's income statement as income (of course!). On that same income statement she'll have many things listed as expenses required to run her business, such as the car she bought.

In the end, this means that Liz's business will pay about $843 of tax on the bonus. So she gets to keep $19,157 of her $20,000 bonus.

That's right, Billy gets to keep $2,297 less of his bonus than Liz does.

"Really?" you're asking. "This is crazy. What's going on?"

Well, business owners make money differently than people with jobs or salaried careers. The systems are set up differently. Remember the story of Ansel from earlier in this book? As he found out when he compared the costs of travel, hotels, and vacations, the system benefits business owners more than people with jobs or careers.

> **Whatever course you take in life, knowing about owner benefits is helpful.**

That's one of the reasons we highly recommended that you consider entrepreneurship. This is true for adults as well as teens. The tax laws are set up in such a way to help businesses prosper, because business success is what drives the whole economy. Because of this, it's very wise for talented, ambitious people to put themselves on the business-ownership side of the tax laws.

A Huge Difference

Note that the numbers we've outlined here will differ a little depending on which province or state you live in. And in some nations, they're very, very different. But in the U.S., this example tells us a lot about how the system works.

All in all, how did the whole thing turn out for Billy and Liz?[**]

BILLY	LIZ'S BUSINESS
-$16,927 cost of car	-$14,630 cost of car
+$16,860 bonus	+$19,157 bonus

At the end, Billy walks away with a Buick and his wallet has $67 less cash than when he started.

In contrast, Liz's company has a Buick and $4,527 more cash than at the beginning.

So, in identical transactions, Liz is ahead of Billy by $4,460. (Again, this is only a fictitious example designed to demonstrate the impact taxes can have on your finances in different scenarios.)

Add up all such transactions over twenty or thirty years of their work lives, and the differences between these ways of earning money become huge. It's often literally in the millions.

It Works

That's why we call this "A Major Secret!" In the United States and many other nations there are numerous special benefits for business owners that people with jobs and salaried careers don't enjoy.

[**]Of course, this is only an example. Taxes are complicated, and there are a lot of laws dealing with them. If you go into business for yourself, you'll definitely want to hire competent accountants and tax advisers.

In some nations, the reason for this is rooted in their aristocratic history. In others, like the U.S., it stems from the high value Americans put on entrepreneurship and free enterprise during the first 150 years after the founding. They knew that business owners create most of the jobs in the nation, and they wanted to make sure that being a business owner remained enticing. After all, it takes a lot of extra work.

Whatever course you take in life, knowing about owner benefits is helpful. If you choose the job or career path, even just running a small side business can help you take advantage of many of these benefits.

This can be a huge help to your finances over time.

YOUTH
Call to Action

A. Describe, in your own words, how business owner benefits work. Discuss this with your parents.

B. Given the "hidden costs" of business owner benefits, why would owning your own business—either full time, or even just on the side—be of value in your life? Discuss this with your parents.

C. Are you staying current on your income statement every month? This will train you to think like an owner.

PARENTS AND OTHER ADULTS
Call to Action

1. Describe, in your own words, how business owner benefits work.

2. Given the "hidden costs" of business owner benefits, why would owning your own business—either full time, or even just on the side—be of value in your life?

3. If you are a parent, discuss items 1 and 2 with your youth.

4. Are you staying current on your income statement every month? This will train you to think like an owner.

"Those who cannot remember the past
are doomed to repeat it...."

TOOL #15

Insurance: Is It an Asset?

*The reason for insurance is to protect you
from financial catastrophe.*
—STANLEY F. SCHMIDT

Yes or No?

One hidden cost that can actually be a positive (if you're smart about it) is insurance. In fact, although insurance may seem like a liability because you have to pay for it each month or year, it can turn out to be a huge asset.

Since unexpected bad things do sometimes happen, insurance is an asset—because eventually you'll probably need it. When you buy insurance, you pay the insurance company a certain amount of money for protection from an accident or catastrophe. For example, if you buy fire insurance for a home you own, and your home has a fire, the insurance company will pay you the amount you were insured to either rebuild the home or make up for your loss.

Insurance companies are able to make a profit because many more people pay for the insurance than experience the disaster—such as a home fire. The same model applies to other types of insurance as well.

The major types of insurance include:

- Vehicle Insurance
- Homeowner's Insurance
- Renter's Insurance
- Health Insurance
- Business Insurance
- Life Insurance

Vehicle Insurance

Most governments require you to have insurance on your car. There are two main types of car insurance. The first one, called *liability* insurance, covers the costs if you are in an accident and people are hurt and/or other cars are damaged. The government usually requires you to carry a minimum amount of liability insurance.

The other kind of car insurance protects your car if it gets damaged. Some people carry what's called *comprehensive* insurance on their car, which means that if the car gets totaled, the insurance company pays to fix or replace it.

If you buy a new car with a loan, your lender will likely require you to have full comprehensive insurance. But if you're a wise buyer and purchased a low mileage used car with cash, you usually don't want to spend the money for full comprehensive insurance. There are slightly cheaper options.

Deductibles: By the way, if you ever need your insurance company to pay the costs of repairs following an accident, you'll have to personally pay the first portion of it, which is called a *deductible.* When you buy insurance, you choose what size deductible you want—usually somewhere between $250 and $1,000 or more. The higher your deductible, the lower the cost of your insurance.

So if your deductible is $500 and you get in a fender bender that is going to cost you $350 to repair, you'll have to cover the cost yourself. If on the other hand it will cost you $2,500, that's why you have insurance. The way it works is that you would pay the first $500 and your insurance company would pay the remaining $2,000.

Plan Car Insurance Wisely: Car accidents do happen. Don't pretend it will never happen to you. It might. Consider if your insurance is what it should be. Is it enough? For example, if you have the bare minimum of car liability insurance required by law, and you get in an accident and someone is really hurt, it can cost many hundreds of thousands of dollars (or more) to fund their medical recovery. Make sure your insurance covers this possibility.

If you don't have good insurance, or enough insurance, you could suffer a major financial hit. Get enough car insurance. Think about it, and take action. After an accident, it's too late.

Homeowner's Insurance

All of this applies to a home you own as well. If you're a teen, you probably don't own any houses yet, but you probably will someday. When you do, insure them well. Insurance is a blessing if you need it. And when you need it, it's one of your most important safety nets.

Again, when you buy a home, take the time to really talk with your insurance agent and learn what you need to know. Don't just take it for granted that the cheapest insurance is enough. It usually isn't. Give this real attention.

If you're buying your home by borrowing money (a loan to buy a property is called a mortgage), the bank or other lender will almost always require you to have good insurance protecting your home. If you buy with cash and own the home outright, you probably won't be required by anyone to insure it, but since it's still a significant asset you'll want to protect it well anyway.

Again, if you chose a high deductible, it will bring your other insurance costs down. Don't forget to also insure the contents of your home; replacing them could be very, very expensive if you have to pay for it all after a disaster. But you don't need to pay extra insurance fees for a bunch of frills. Remember, the purpose of insurance is to protect against financial catastrophe.

If you do business in your home, you'll want an extra business policy that protects against business liability.

Renter's Insurance

If you rent the place where you live, your landlord likely has insurance to cover the home or apartment building, but he usually won't carry insurance for the things you own. If you want to insure your belongings, you'll need to buy your own renter's insurance.

Whether or not this is worth the money depends on what you own. If the loss of your things would be a major financial catastrophe, you'll probably want renter's insurance. If not, don't waste your money.

For young people who rent, this type of insurance is seldom worthwhile. Again, it all depends on what you own.

Health Insurance

Health insurance protects you if you or a member of your family gets sick or hurt and needs medical or hospital care. If this happens, you'll pay the amount of the deductible you chose for your insurance policy, and the insurance company will pay for other expenses (up to the full amount insured).

The needs for health insurance differ a lot between families. The best advice we can give is to follow the general rules of good insurance. As a teen, your insurance is part of your parents' policy—in most cases. Talk to them about what health insurance you have.

If you are a young adult, you might not think much about health insurance because you are young, healthy, and still boast the fearlessness of youth. As you begin building a family, you'll want to do your best to make sure you are covered with at least the basics.

In most cases, it's best to have at least a major medical policy for your family. This means that if something drastic happens to someone in your family, you'll pay a high deductible (like $5,000 or $10,000), and the rest of the care will be covered. Sometimes this renews annually, so check your health care policy before you buy it.

In some nations the government handles health care and takes it from the tax receipts of the nation. If you live in such a country, you are already paying for your health care through your taxes.

Business Insurance

If you own a business, you'll want to make sure any business assets are wisely insured as well (cars, buildings, rented offices, etc.). If you have lots of assets, get liability insurance (both personal and business, as needed) to protect them. Some people engage in lawsuits in order to take your business or personal assets, even if their claims aren't true or justified.[11] This is one of the challenges of being in business sometimes.

Life Insurance

Life insurance is a bit different from the other types of insurance we've discussed so far, because it can be both a protection against catastrophe and an effective long-term investment strategy. The main idea of life insurance is to leave your family with assets if an adult dies and can't continue to care for loved ones. People usually buy such insurance while they are healthy, as a protection against unexpected death.

There are two basic types of life insurance: (1) term life, and (2) permanent life. Term life insurance gives financial help to your family or whomever you designate as the recipient of your life insurance money (called a *beneficiary*) if you die. Term life insurance coverage is relatively inexpensive, but it times out when you get old.

Permanent life insurance (sometimes called "whole life" or "universal life") provides a death benefit plus the cash value you build up as you pay for your life insurance over the years. Different policies build up or guarantee differing amounts of money over time. Permanent life insurance is also a great way to grow your wealth tax free, and there are ways to live off this wealth later in life. So permanent life insurance is not only about protecting your family if the primary income earner dies, but also about investing.

Anyone starting a family should probably get some term insurance right away—to cover at least the primary income earner. Then begin consistently building a permanent life policy as soon as possible.

YOUTH
Call to Action

A. What is the purpose of insurance?

B. What is a deductible? What is the benefit of a high deductible?

C. When should you get more car insurance? (Answer: when not having it could result in a financial catastrophe.)

D. When should you get insurance of any kind? (Answer: when not having it could result in a financial catastrophe.)

E. Talk to your parents about car, homeowner, renter, health, business, and life insurance. What do you have? What do you need?

PARENTS AND OTHER ADULTS
Call to Action

1. What is the purpose of insurance?

2. What is the benefit of a high deductible?

3. When should you get more car insurance? (Answer: when not having it could result in a financial catastrophe.)

4. When should you get insurance of any kind? (Answer: when not having it could result in a financial catastrophe.)

5. What car, homeowner, renter, health, business, and/or life insurance (if any) do you have? What do you wisely need—to protect against a financial catastrophe? What are you doing to take advantage of the wealth-building advantages in some types of life insurance policies?

"The tide waits for no man...."

The Problem with Investments (and How to Overcome It)

To the nimble go the spoils.
—KEN FAVARO

Mastering Your Field

To be really good at something takes time. This is true for carpenters, accountants, actors, entrepreneurs, engineers, pilots, athletes, and on and on. There is a reason that beginners need time to learn, make mistakes, improve, and get better at what they do.

Best-selling author Malcolm Gladwell argued that it takes about 10,000 hours of focus on a career field to really become good at it. This applies to most aspects of human endeavor.

For example, the best brain surgeon in North America has spent countless hours in school and in the operating room, learning, studying, practicing, and implementing his skills. He or she is highly trained, highly skilled, highly intelligent, and highly qualified. Yet imagine that you are boarding a military jet to ride as a passenger on a quick flight across the ocean. The engines are firing, the pilot tells you he's almost ready for takeoff, and you strap in.

Then you ask who did the last mechanical check on the jet. The pilot tells you that the last three checks were done by the best brain surgeon in North America. He was visiting for a couple of weeks, and since he is so good with brains, the officers just decided to put him in charge of all aircraft maintenance.

How do you feel about this?

On the one hand, you hope nothing was wrong with the jet to begin with. But on the other hand, you're starting to sweat. This is a very high tech, hugely complex machine, and the last person to check it out and give you the go-ahead is a complete amateur—at least when it comes to jets.

Or imagine that you're entering the hospital for brain surgery, and the jet's pilot comes up and tells you he's your surgeon. "Just trying out something new today," he says cheerfully. "If I like it, maybe I'll switch careers."

"He's an amazingly well-trained pilot," your nurse assures you. "One of the best in the world. You're in good hands."

Being highly skilled, deeply experienced, and extremely good at one thing doesn't make you good at everything.

The point here is obvious. Being highly skilled, deeply experienced, and extremely good at one thing doesn't make you good at everything. And all of this applies to investing.

Investing means taking the money you've built up in your savings, or from your other work and businesses, and doing something with it that creates increased assets. And just like being a brain surgeon or a pilot, or having one of many other occupations, the best investors have learned over long periods of time through hard work and tenacity, mistakes and corrections, effort and experience.

Don't Invest in Things You Don't Understand

To put our point simply: If you haven't put in your "10,000 hours" learning how to invest and practicing investment with a lot of success, you're probably not very good at it. And even if you do it well for a time, your lack of experience and skill will eventually show. If you have assets, you've almost certainly worked hard to earn and save your assets, and turning them over to an amateur investor (even if that amateur investor is you) is a bad idea.

This is the problem with most investing. The best investors know the best investments, because they know what they're doing. The rest of the people are amateurs.

But guess what? It seems that almost nobody wants to hear this about investing. The strange truth is that many of the same people who only want the well-trained pilot to fly their jet, and the world-class brain surgeon to cut into their brain, somehow take a different approach when it comes to investing.

> **If you haven't put in your "10,000 hours" learning how to invest and practicing investment with a lot of success, you're probably not very good at it. And even if you do it well for a time, your lack of experience and skill will eventually show.**

They think they'll be good at it. After all, they've made money doing what they do—whatever their profession. Why wouldn't they be good at investing as well? Or at least, a lot of people think this way.

If you invest in a field that you haven't put in the 10,000 or more hours to learn and master, you'll probably lose your shirt. This is perhaps the main problem with investment. Everyone seems to say that you should do it ("Invest in a bunch of things, the more diverse the better—just get online and start trading. It's fun!"), but they're wrong. If you don't know what you're doing—if you don't really, deeply know the field and business and people you're investing in—you're really just gambling.

Now, if you do know the field extremely well, that's a different story. That's your profession. You've put in your 10,000 hours—or maybe a lot more. But if not, beware.

Any investment in something you really don't know much about is a lot like the story of "the old woman who triumphantly announced that she had borrowed enough money to pay all her debts."[12] Funny, right?

Not for her. If she borrowed it, she's still in just as much debt. And depending on interest rates and the fees associated with her new loan, she might be in *more* debt. Don't invest in what you don't fully understand.

Carly's Plan

When Carly first started making a lot of profit from her business, she received a number of calls from people wanting to meet with her about what they called "an upscale investment." Happily situated in her new home on the hill, she felt flattered by this attention, and by some of the people who called her (well-known former politicians, retired professional athletes, and some of the most famous people in the city). She said yes.

But something happened during the meetings Carly and her husband held with these people. At first, she felt honored to be on their radar. Then, as they outlined their proposals and asked if she wanted to be in on the ground floor of their various projects, she started to realize that she didn't understand the details very well.

She didn't want to disappoint such people, so she smiled, nodded, and asked them how much they would need. By the time the meetings were winding down, Carly didn't feel like she could say no without being seen as small or unsophisticated in their eyes. Her husband always said, "Thank you for the opportunity. We'll think about it."

But after they left, Carly always felt that if they didn't invest, they'd lose the respect of these famous people. She always called them back the next day and agreed to invest. She was caught in a serious status trap.

At first, the investments mostly consisted of $10,000 here and $12,000 there. This was hard on her business cash flow, but she shrugged it off as a kind of public relations expense. This was pure justification, but she didn't know what else to do.

Word got out that she was an easy target for such investments, and the amounts rose over time. This nearly ran her business into

> "Only invest money you can afford to lose entirely in speculations outside your area(s) of mastery. Only invest a little, if any, in such ventures."

the ground even before the construction market experienced a recession.

During all this time, Carly only got her money back on one of the investments. A successful architect in town, and a former mayor, came to dinner at her home and told her that he had done due diligence and decided not to complete the planned downtown renovation after all. He refunded her $5,000 check on the spot. With that exception, all the other "investments" bore no fruit.

This Really Matters!

As Chris Brady and Orrin Woodward put it: "Only invest money you can afford to lose entirely in speculations outside your area(s) of mastery. Only invest a little, if any, in such ventures."[13] Likewise, one of the most successful investors in history, Warren Buffett, made the large majority of his investments in his own company, Berkshire Hathaway. He taught that focusing your investments in your own business, in something you really, truly, know and understand, is a key to wise investment.[14]

One account in *U.S. News and World Report* summarized Buffett's investment strategy as follows:

- Research extensively
- Buy what you know
- Resist peer pressure
- Shun risk
- Learn from your mistakes
- Eliminate debt[15]

"Buying what you know" means only investing in the things you understand. If you haven't gained "10,000 hour" mastery in anything, save your money and invest in your own knowledge and your own business. Once you've gained real mastery, invest in the things you know—mainly your own business, if you have one.

When You Don't Know

For example: Excited about the sale of their second home, Matt and Latticia decided that real estate was a good investment for them. They had purchased three homes total—the one they still lived in, the starter home where they had lived for six years, and a second home they bought and sold within a few years.

They were enthused, so they researched and purchased another home as a rental property to produce more income. During the eight years they owned the house, they only rented it for a total of a few months. The rest of the time it sat vacant. Part of the reason for this was they bought the house in a town several hours drive from their own. It had better prices than their own city, so they felt they were getting a bargain.

The other reason they didn't rent it very often is that the first family to rent it did a lot of damage to the home. Of course, from their distant city they didn't know this was happening until the renters moved out. They paid late over half of the time and then stopped paying.

When Latticia called friends in the town for help, they drove past the home and found that it was vacant. Matt hired a handyman to put the house back in ship-shape for the next renter and was soon informed that the house would require thousands of dollars of repairs.

> **"Buying what you know" means only investing in the things you understand. If you haven't gained "10,000 hour" mastery in anything, save your money and invest in your own knowledge and your own business.**

For a while, Matt and Latticia just let it sit vacant while they grappled with what to do. Eventually they told the handyman to go ahead and fix it. He did, and it ended up costing even more than they had originally thought.

It needed a new cooler, the heaters were broken and had leaked on the wood floors in three of the four bedrooms, and some of the windows were broken. It looked like neighborhood kids had seen the vacant house and used it to practice throwing rocks through most of the windows that weren't visible from the main street.

When the project was complete, Matt and Latticia were still ahead a few hundred dollars from the year's rent, but the house was hardly the income producer they had planned on.

They debated about what to do. Sometimes they felt that they should rent it again. "Not all renters are like that, right?" they asked themselves. Other times they worried that they didn't want to go through that kind of hassle again. They were busy raising their family and building their main business, and managing renters from hours away felt like a major imposition.

After it sat empty for three years, they put the house on the market. It remained empty for three more years. During all this time they had to pay the taxes, periodic repairs and upkeep, and base utilities. When the house eventually sold, they had spent more on it than they ever took in from rent.

This true story illustrates how difficult it can be to invest in a field you haven't mastered. A full-time real estate owner would have had a very different experience, because he would have approached the whole project differently. But when people try to invest outside their area(s) of mastery, they nearly always fail to make the venture profitable or enjoyable.

The solution? Invest in what you know.

YOUTH
Call to Action

A. Do you ever find yourself in a status trap? What should you do when this happens?

B. Why do you think so many broke people suggest investing in a lot of fields without really understanding what you are doing? Could it be that they're not following one of these essential guidelines:

- Research extensively
- Buy what you know
- Resist peer pressure
- Shun risk
- Learn from your mistakes
- Eliminate debt

C. What business fields do you know at a level of 10,000 hours experience? Write them down:

PARENTS AND OTHER ADULTS
Call to Action

1. Do you ever find yourself in a status trap? What should you do when this happens?

2. Why do you think so many broke people suggest investing in a lot of fields without really understanding what you are doing? Could it be that they're not following one of these essential guidelines:

- Research extensively
- Buy what you know
- Resist peer pressure
- Shun risk
- Learn from your mistakes
- Eliminate debt

3. What business fields do you know at a level of 10,000 hours experience? Write them down:

"Time is money...."

TOOL #17

How to Invest

You don't know what you don't know....
—ANONYMOUS

*For those with poor financial discipline,
a lack of money is not the problem,
therefore more money is not the solution.*
—CHRIS BRADY

How to Invest Wisely and Effectively

When you invest in what you know, your investments are much more effective. In fact, Chris Brady and Orrin Woodward outlined a hierarchy of good investment, which teaches us how to focus on excellent, high quality investing. This hierarchy includes 7 Levels of investing, and knowing what to do in each of the Levels is a powerful financial tool.

Let's learn about each of the 7 Levels of investing.

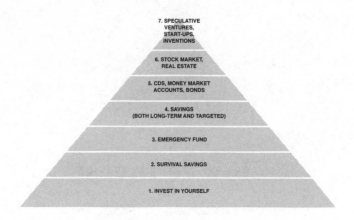

Level 1. Invest in Yourself

This is the base level of the hierarchy and therefore the most important. It includes investing in your own knowledge by reading, reading, reading. Be a voracious reader! Fill your mind with knowledge. Read, read, read. This is an excellent investment in you.

> **When you invest in what you know, your investments are much more effective.**

By the way, do this as much as possible while you're young. And keep doing it throughout life. Leaders are readers, as Harry Truman put it.

Investing in yourself also means learning as much financial wisdom as you can. For example, you'll learn an incredible amount by keeping your income statements up to date every month. As we've discussed, this teaches you invaluable lessons about money and leadership.

Also learn to consistently develop your strengths and overcome your weaknesses. Everything you do to improve yourself is an investment in you.

Starting your own business is also a major investment in yourself. This is true of smaller, practice businesses you initiate in your youth and other, bigger-scale businesses you build over the course of years. Building a business is a huge investment in you.

To put it bluntly: investing in you is the first and most important level of investment you can ever make. Get good at it, and never quit doing it. The best, most successful entrepreneurs, business owners, and other leaders almost all still read, read, read, and learn, learn, learn—even though they've already achieved great success. Always keep investing in you.

Your Own Business

Another way to invest in yourself is to invest some of your savings in your own business. Is there a way that some extra cash would greatly help your business grow and increase its profits? This can be tricky, so ask yourself the following questions before you put savings into your business:

- Do you know your business well enough to know that your savings won't be wasted? Do you have a mentor who knows your business even better than you and can help you weigh this decision?
- How do you know that using your savings to build your business will bring more assets and increase your income? How do you know it won't just fail? Don't ever speculate with your savings. Use it only to buy true, proven assets. (If you know your business well enough, or your mentor or parents know it well enough, you'll know what ways of investing savings money in your own business definitely

205

work. Take your time, and make sure you know what will work before using savings.)

- Have you done this before with a small amount and turned it into a true success? If not, it might be best to start very small and try it out before you use bigger amounts of money.

When you do invest savings money wisely in your own business and follow through effectively, it creates bigger and more valuable assets than it does just sitting in the bank.

One of the best ways to invest some of your savings is in your own business.

Never forget that this is the purpose of investing: to build your assets.

Level 2. Invest in an Emergency Fund

We've already discussed this, but it's very important. It's also the second level of wise and effective investing. As mentioned, every time you earn any money, put some of it in an emergency fund. And don't spend it unless you face a real emergency.

Every time you earn any money, put some of it in an emergency fund. And don't spend it unless you face a real emergency.

Likewise, if you do spend some or all of it on an emergency, quickly rebuild the fund. Always have an emergency fund that you can turn to in a time of need. This rainy day fund is one of the most important of all investments. If you don't have it, build it right away.

206

Your emergency fund should have enough money to cover around 3–4 months of your normal expenses. For youth that might be around $400, or even more or less than this. For many adults, build your emergency fund until you have at least $1,000 in it, and then keep building it to at least $5,000.

Of course, if your monthly expenses are $10,000, you'll want to create an emergency fund much bigger than $5,000. The idea is to build an emergency fund big enough to cover 3–6 months of your living expenses.

Level 3. Invest in Sensible Survival Prep

This might sound strange, but disasters do sometimes happen. Be prepared. We're not suggesting that you go off the deep end and create a mountain compound to wait out a "zombie apocalypse." Not at all. We're recommending a wise preparation plan in case you really need it someday.

What would such preparation consist of? Well, think of what you would need in your area if you experienced a major flood, a power outage that lasted for weeks or more, or an earthquake, tornado, hurricane, or other serious disaster.

Start by stashing "some cash in a safe, secure, secret place." Teens, coordinate this with your parents. Adults will probably want to put away some gold and silver in case inflation totally ruins the currency. Silver is good for easy exchange and reliable purchasing, and gold is an unshakable (and non-tamperable) store of value.

As the *Financial Fitness* book put it: "By the way, don't be too extreme about this. We are not doom and gloomers, and we're not predicting a world with roving bandits and no electricity.

It could happen, but so could a lot of things. We are simply suggesting that part of sound money planning is to realize that bank holidays and closed banks can happen."[16] A little preparation beforehand will go a long way if you ever need it.

Level 4. Invest in Savings

Start saving right now. Don't wait to begin saving. As we discussed in earlier chapters, start saving a prearranged percentage of every bit of money you bring in from now on. Never skip this. Never rationalize it away.

These first four levels of investment may just be the most important. They give you a foundation of assets: a better you, an emergency fund, items to help get you through a major disaster, and a growing savings that will help build your assets for the rest of your life.

Don't take financial advice from people who haven't succeeded financially in the way you want to do. Take this advice from Brady and Woodward: Don't invest in Levels 5 or above (on the hierarchy) until you've done Levels 1 through 4.

All of this applies to teens as well as adults. Teens will want to coordinate with their parents on all of these investments.

Level 5. Secure Investments

We're going to speak directly to teens here, but most of what we say applies to adults as well. Teens: As you build up more and more savings you'll reach a point where it doesn't make sense to leave so much money in a regular savings account. If you leave it there, you'll only earn a very small percent return on it. You can do better.

CDs

For example, we've already talked about CDs. You can make at least a little more interest on your savings by putting some of it into CDs. See what rates your bank pays, and compare with other banks. Shop around. Be sure to discuss what you're doing with your parents, and keep them involved in the process.

Remember that CDs keep your money for a set period of time, usually from 6 months to 5 years, so be smart about what CDs you use. Think through the details before you sign up.

But if you're just going to leave your money sitting there in a savings account, you can put some of it in CDs and get paid more. Make sure you leave some of your savings in a regular account where you will have access to it if needed.

By this point you're a proven saver, or you wouldn't have enough in savings to even be talking about CDs. Congratulations. However, CDs are usually a pretty poor investment because the rates of return are so low and they tie up your money.

Money Market Accounts

These have some of the benefits of both checking and savings accounts. You can write checks against your balance, although this is usually limited to a few checks per month. Like a savings account, money market accounts (also known as MMAs), earn interest. In fact, they usually earn higher rates than regular savings accounts, but the interest rate fluctuates, usually daily.

The downside is that most MMAs require a higher minimum balance, meaning that you are required to leave a minimum of anywhere from $1,000 to $25,000 in the account (depending on the bank) in order to earn interest and avoid monthly fees.

Because you can write checks on money market accounts, you can get your money out whenever you choose.

Bonds

Another kind of secure investment comes in the form of bonds. A bond is basically just a promise note that guarantees your money back plus interest at a certain future date. A "municipal bond" means it is backed (or promised) by a municipality such as a city government. A treasury bond is backed by the U.S. Treasury. There are many other types of bonds as well.

When you put money in a bond, it acts like a CD. You put it in for a preset amount of time, and you get paid a preset rate of interest. But you can't take your money out until the agreed upon time without paying a penalty. In some cases you can't take it out at all until the term of the bond is complete. So the interest rate of the bond is fixed (which is why they are called "fixed income"). But because bonds can be bought or sold, their prices fluctuate according to the whims of the bond market.

But there are other ways to buy bonds. There are companies that lump a bunch of bonds together and then allow investors to buy into these accounts. These are called "bond mutual funds." The advantage of these is that they allow you to put your money in or take it out any time. You can benefit from the money or "yield" that the bonds pay without having to hold them for the whole term of any individual bond. But as with individual bonds, the value of these funds fluctuates with the market.

Bonds (and bond funds) are generally considered a very safe form of investing, and they generally perform best in bad economic times.

When you are looking at bonds, compare the interest rates they pay to those of CDs. Since both of these are generally secure, you'll often want to go for the best rate. Be sure to talk about this with your parents, and get the help of an expert investor who can tell you the pitfalls and reputation of any given bond you decide to invest in.

Level 6. Real Estate and Stocks

As for Level 6 and 7 investments, heed our warning: Tread carefully.

In fact, we'll make this very simple. If your primary business is real estate, and you've put in the 10,000 or more hours to master it, you don't need us telling you whether or not it's a good investment. You're the expert on this, so you know what works and what doesn't.

But if real estate isn't your business, steer carefully. When you buy your own home, get help from a wise person you trust who really understands the field of real estate. If you buy real estate for your business, do the same.

But don't take your hard-earned money from your primary business and throw it away on real estate investments just because a lot of people say this is a good idea. It's a good idea for those who understand the field, for those with the 10,000 hours of experience and wisdom. It's a good idea for those who know how to tell if a specific house, building, business complex, or plot of land is a good investment—or not.

As we've already said, if this isn't your profession, it's not a good idea for you. Also, if you are not going to be in full control over whether the investment succeeds or not, realize that this is risky.

The very same thing applies to stocks. There are two definitions that are helpful here:

First, stocks (also called "equities") consist of ownership in a company. When you purchase a stock, you are purchasing a share of ownership in that company. In fact, when you buy a stock, the company gives you a paper showing your ownership—and the paper itself is called a "stock certificate." But actually it is just proof of the stock you own, your little piece of ownership in the company.

The business then takes the money you paid for the stock and uses it to try to grow and/or improve its operations. When the business makes a profit, it divides the profits between the stockholders, and you get paid your share—whatever your percentage of the company's total stock. The little bit of money they pay you is called a "dividend."

Second, stock markets (also called "stock exchanges") are made up of buyers and sellers of stock. Some stock markets facilitate most of their trading online, but the large ones also provide a place for big buyers and sellers to make their exchanges in person, as at the New York Stock Exchange. The buying and selling must be done through stockbrokers or an online brokerage account.

If your profession is the stock market, and you've learned your 10,000 hours of wisdom, okay. You know when and where and how to make this work.

If not, you don't. Be careful. Also, there are many great (and free) educational services you can take advantage of that allow you to simulate the buying and selling of stocks. Besides being a lot of fun, these simulations are a great way to learn how the markets work.

Mutual Funds, Real Estate Investment Trusts (REITs), and ETFs

What exactly are mutual funds? Put simply, mutual funds are investment opportunities run by companies who manage many different stocks, bonds, and other types of investments. You put your money in their fund, and they use your money to invest in a whole assortment of specific stocks and/or bonds.

You can keep an eye on your account to see whether the value of your investments goes up or down, but you don't get to pick individual stocks to buy or sell. The professional fund managers handle those choices. Sometimes a certain mutual fund does well one year, only to lose money the next year. Other times a mutual fund will do well for several years or poorly for several years.

Real estate offers a similar option called Real Estate Investment Trusts (REITs). When you invest money in an REIT, you aren't the sole owner of a certain piece of land or a home or shopping center. You share ownership with everyone else who has invested in the same REIT (which owns a whole bunch of properties). A manager chooses which pieces of property to buy and sell, the amount to charge for rent, etc, and you simply watch to see if your investment goes up or down.

Stocks, mutual funds, and REITs are instruments that allow you to easily own a slice of something bigger. In the case of a stock (or mutual funds), you are owning a slice of a bigger company or companies. In the case of an REIT, you are owning a slice of a collection of real estate. Stocks and REITs are easily traded on exchanges, where market forces can quickly determine their value.

Exchange Traded Funds, or ETFs, are simply mutual funds that are bought and sold like a stock on the stock exchange. ETFs have gotten popular over recent years because they are so easy to buy and sell. Ultimately, though, they are mutual funds made up of an assortment of stock, or bonds, or whatever.

If you want this to be your profession, start working in it and learning. Put in enough time to really know what works and what doesn't work. In the words of Brady and Woodward: "Become a master." Otherwise, don't invest in it unless you can afford to lose what you put in, or at least until you can educate yourself enough to understand the risks and rewards involved.

The general rule for new categories of investment that you're just learning:

1-Only invest money you can afford to entirely lose.
2-Only invest a little at first.

If you follow these two hard and fast rules, one of two things will most likely happen. Either you'll lose your money and decide that the real estate or stock market isn't as much fun as you once imagined. Or you'll learn important lessons that become part of your 10,000 hours and you'll keep studying and learning in order to master this new field.

Finally, concerning all investments: Always strive to invest like the wealthy (in things you already really know and understand), and live like the middle class—frugally, ignoring status, avoiding debt, and always building assets. This is a powerful combination for financial success and happiness.

Level 7. Other Speculation

The 7th Level usually occurs when you have some money (because you've saved and built up assets). When you arrive at this point, a lot of people will naturally come to you hoping you'll invest in their "exciting new project." This might be a new idea, a start-up company, an invention, or something else.

The first step in considering this kind of investment is to ask, "How well do I know this field?" If you don't know it, don't invest in it.

If you do know it, and know it well, you'll be able to quickly identify how well the presenter has prepared, if he has a likely "winner" for a project or not, and what holes he has in his plan. If you know the field well, these things will be obvious to you.

If you don't, don't invest in it.

Why? Because those 10,000 hours are going to teach you things that are absolutely essential for investing success. For example, let's say your sister comes to you and says she wants to build an ice cream shop in Washington D.C. and hopes you will invest $10,000 in it. She's planning to get your parents and her parents-in-law to invest $10,000 each as well. She's run the numbers, and she's pretty sure this will work.

If you don't know this business, you can't be sure what's going to happen. But she's your sister, so you decide to help.

Guess what? You just lost $10,000.

If you know the ice cream shop market in Washington, you know such a start-up has cost around $120,000 in the recent past.[17] If you are familiar with this market, you know that she'll likely need three times as many employees in the summer as in the winter.[18] Does she know this? Probably not. Or maybe she does. But if you know enough to ask her this question, you'll quickly get a sense for how well she's likely to do

> **The first step in considering this kind of investment is to ask, "How well do I know this field?" If you don't know it very, very well, don't invest in it. If you do know it, and know it well, you'll be able to quickly identify how well the presenter has prepared.**

If you know this field, you'll know that in some winter months she might only pull in about $6,000 in sales—but she'll probably make that much on some *days* in the summer.[19] If you don't know any of these things, you're throwing away your money. Given the realities of the market, the $10,000 likely won't even get her started, and you'll probably never see it again, or worse, she'll come back later asking for more so she "won't lose the original $10,000!"

Another example. Rita started a private high school from scratch, built it up for fifteen years, and then retired. Eventually she decided she wanted to help other people build such schools around North America. She did this for several years, and had huge success. Then she retired for good.

Later her sister Judy contacted her and told Rita that she too was building a private school—this one an elementary. She asked for help funding the start-up, and Rita agreed to meet with her and discuss it.

As Rita read through the proposal during the meeting, she noticed something strange. "Why do you have both a principal and a CEO?" she asked. Judy replied that the CEO would run the administration and the principal would focus on the academics.

With twenty years of experience running and consulting with successful schools, Rita knew this was a concern. She had seen it before, and she knew just what to ask. "Which one of them is in charge?"

"Uh—" Judy hesitated. "They're both in charge. The CEO is over administrative issues, and the principal is in charge of academics."

"But when a really important issue comes up, and all the faculty and parents are split on how it should go, which one makes the final decision—CEO or principal?"

Judy was getting frustrated. "It depends. If it's academic, the principal is in charge...."

Rita smiled to reassure her sister and said, "I've seen this done several times, and one of the people always ends up in charge. If it's the principal, that's great—because schools are about academics. But if it's the CEO, your school will struggle."

Judy was hesitant, but she listened respectfully.

"How much are you paying each of them?" Rita asked.

Judy thumbed through her notes, then said, "The principal is making $48,000 a year, and the CEO is getting $85,000."

Rita's jaw dropped. She knew right then that she couldn't invest in Judy's school. She knew the numbers for private schools, and she knew that this disparity was way out of bounds. The CEO would always be in charge. She tried to give her sister as much advice as Judy would accept, but she declined to invest.

If Rita hadn't known the details, she might have invested— and lost her money when Judy's school shut down just two years later. Only invest in what you know.

Remember, most people are broke! Listen to those who have the kind of money you want to have, not to people who are struggling financially. Again, here's how Brady and Woodward put it: "Only invest money you can afford to lose entirely in speculations outside your area(s) of mastery. Only invest a little, if any, in such ventures."[20]

The investment problem is real. If investment isn't your primary business, focus on investing in Levels 1–4. And sometimes Level 5 and carefully in Level 6. Build these into the very best assets you can.

YOUTH
Call to Action

A. Always remember that the real key to all investing is to minimize any investments in anything except things you know about.

B. Look at your Level 1–4 investing. How are you doing? Discuss it with your parents. Make a list of ways you might improve it. How can you begin learning about Levels 5 and 6?

C. Based on your list, make a plan to do even better. Implement it.

PARENTS AND OTHER ADULTS
Call to Action

1.   Always remember that the real key to all investing is to minimize any investments in anything except things you know about.

2.   Look at your Level 1–4 investing. How are you doing? Make a list of ways you might improve it. How can you begin learning about Levels 5 and 6?

3.   Based on your list, make a plan to do even better. Implement it

"Call a spade a spade...."

Thinking *Inside* the Box

Owning a rental house, owning things you can touch (such as gold), owning a business—these are things you can put your hands on. Paper assets feel different. You can choose your adjective: airy, ethereal, ghostlike, insubstantial.
—STANLEY F. SCHMIDT

Most of us started with no cash and no connections.
True entrepreneurs find a way.
Those who aren't true entrepreneurs find excuses.
—MARK CUBAN

How to Think!

A lot of business books talk about the importance of "thinking outside the box." This means rather than getting caught in the same old views and stale thinking of the past, instead looking for new, better ways of thinking and doing things. But as one business thinker realized, the best way to "think outside the box" is to learn to really "think *inside* the box."[21]

If you like riddles, you'll love this. If not, it's still pretty fun. As best-selling author Stephen Palmer wrote: "Thinking outside the box, we've been told, is the path to boundless creativity and record-shattering innovation." But "[i]n fact, it is…limitations and constraints that spark our most creative ideas and generate the most practical and innovative solutions. Our constraints hold the key to our freedom."[22]

What does this mean, exactly? Palmer continued: "Consider an exercise: For which of the following two challenges could you generate the most practical, implementable [and innovative, creative] ideas in ten minutes:

"1-Create a business.

"2-Create…[a] business that:
*Leverages your particular interests and passions…
*Requires no more than $1,000 to start.
*Can be operated in 10 hours per week or less.
*Can eventually generate at least $2,000…net profit per month."[23]

Clearly the second option is much easier to imagine and create. As a result, you're a lot more likely to really get what you want if you use option 2 (or something like it, with the specific things you want from your business) than if you just flail around trying to figure out option 1.

> **"Our constraints hold the key to our freedom."**

What Kind of Business Would You Like?

Let's take a few minutes and do option 2 of this exercise. But instead of just using this list of what the business should be like, write your own. For example:

- It must be interesting to you. What kinds of businesses would meet this requirement? Write them below. Just brainstorm—it's okay to list a few or a lot.

_____

_____

_____

_____

_____

_____

_____

_____

- What value can you think of bringing to customers? Or what pain that people are experiencing can you eliminate? Truly successful businesses meet a real need or fix a real problem.

_____

_____

_____

_____

_____

_____

_____

- How much is the most you would want to spend on starting it?

_____

_____

_____

_____

_____

_____

- How much time would you want to spend on it each week? How much is too much? How much is too little?

_____

_____

_____

_____

_____

- How much do you want it to make per month? You don't have to be specific, but try to get close.

_____

_____

_____

_____

_____

It Really Works

The exercise above is an excellent way to start thinking about your entrepreneurial options. If you choose to take the job or career path in life, such entrepreneurial thinking will still help you be a better leader and innovator.

The reason "thinking inside the box" works is that when we narrow our focus, we start to focus. Without getting specific, there's usually no real focus at all.

In educational psychology, this is known as the "zone of optimal confusion."[24] This simply means that when students, teens, and even adults know exactly what is expected of them, they usually aren't very creative. On the other extreme, if they have *no idea* what is expected, they're not very creative either.

> The reason "thinking inside the box" works is that when we narrow our focus, we actually start to focus. Without getting specific, there's usually no real focus at all.

Human creativity sparks and flourishes when we are a little confused. If we know some of the goals, some of the expectations, but not everything, we're a lot more creative. We're not sure what to do, but we do know certain things that must be done and other things that should not be done.

In such an environment, we are able to open our minds, see what is needed, and then figure out creative and innovative ways to go about getting it. This is also known simply as "learning." When we're not thinking this way, very little learning takes place.

This is why, though memorization in school and other educational pursuits can help us store facts, equations, quotes, and even ideas, we aren't really *thinking* until we have to apply those ideas in some meaningful way. This is key to financial fitness and leadership, because the best leaders know the details and the principles, but they also know how to *think* about them innovatively.

Another phrase for this is "desirable difficulties,"[25] or challenges that make us think more deeply and respond with creativity and innovation. Leaders spend their lives dealing with such challenges and projects. This is a huge part of what makes them leaders, because most people don't spend their whole life trying to overcome such difficulties. But leaders do.

Leaders spend their lives dealing with such challenges and projects.

Indeed, this is one of the reasons that the tools in this book are so helpful, because many of them, like the income statement entries every month, train people to think far beyond the norm. This is powerful preparation for leadership and true financial fitness.

A simpler way to say all this is that to become a leader you need to push yourself outside your usual comfort zone.

Why This Matters So Much

The reason we are making such a point of this is that some experts say today's teens and young adults are very weak in this skill—pushing beyond their comfort zones.[26] This is often lacking in millennials and postmillennials. If you're a teen, or soon will be, this is very important. And it's just as essential to know this if you're an adult, because you'll be working with millennials and postmillennials for the rest of your life.

Especially for Teens

But what, exactly, do these labels mean? "Millennial generation" is the name our society has given to people born between the early 1980s thru the early 2000s. And postmillennials are those who were born in the early 2000s and since.

In comparison to millennials and postmillennials, people born from the late 1940s thru the mid 1960s are called the baby boomers, and those born in the mid 1960s thru the early 1980s are referred to as Generation X. In other words, today's teens and young adults are all either millennials or postmillennials.

But why does this matter? The answer is simple: knowing your generation's major tendencies will help you make better leadership and financial decisions. More specifically, since doing things beyond their comfort zone is a serious struggle for many millennials and postmillennials, a lot of them are likely to make bad financial decisions.

But not you. You're not just any millennial or postmillennial; you're growing up to be one of the leaders. This means you need to be even better at applying the tools and principles of financial fitness, because you need to show and teach others in your generation how to do it. This is a huge advantage.

Entitlement

In addition to struggling with pushing themselves, many in these two generations are also known for feeling and acting "entitled."[27] This means that many of your peers feel that money should just be given to them—like the story of Tom earlier in this book demanding that his father send him money for his car payment.

You know that such entitlement is misguided, and as a leader in your generation your example is needed. In fact, this feeling of entitlement is very widespread. For example, one group of teens and young adults was interviewed about whether they approved of the government using our military in other nations. The numbers were high.

But when the same youth were asked if they would go and serve in the military, the numbers were extremely low. In other words, many millennials and postmillennials want the U.S. to use its power, but they don't want to be personally involved or put in danger. This is what entitlement is all about.

The Solution Is Service!

As leaders in these generations, you will need to understand how to be financially fit, how to be an effective leader, and how to work in teams. These skills are simply essential. The truth is that they have always been vital in leadership, but as the millennial and postmillennial generations increase in numbers and influence, more such leaders will be needed.

> As leaders in these generations, you will need to understand how to be financially fit, how to be an effective leader, and how to work in teams.

Perhaps the greatest solution to these two major challenges faced by millennials and postmillennials is that they are also known as very giving generations.[28] This means that they genuinely care about people and want to help others succeed. Wherever you make your living in the decades ahead (job, career, or business ownership), service is going to be at the core of any success you achieve. Further, you will want to have an eye for social causes and charitable impact.

Again, this has always been true of great leadership. But it is even more significant given the culture of these two rising generations. The tools outlined in this book will help you be a better leader and example as you apply them and as you always see your work as true service.

Many, many millennial and postmillennial entrepreneurs have gone online to tackle major world problems, from war and hunger to the poverty that comes when national policies drive away many of the jobs. There are literally thousands of online projects run by young people from these two generations, and many of them are making a huge difference.

For example, some of them have helped provide water for thousands of people in Africa who simply did not have a good water source. Others combine travel with service, often called "voluntourism."[29] This allows people to travel, tour new areas of the world, and work on service projects while they are on vacation. There are many other examples.

But this isn't limited to philanthropy. Many young business owners are combining their passions with profits and building effective companies that often do even more for needy people than charities. For example, giving people jobs or helping them start businesses is nearly always a much bigger service to their lives and needs than simply sending them boxes of food.

Both are good, certainly. But providing much-needed jobs and business ownership opportunities in developing nations provides more help to the economy than almost anything else. Without such jobs and business owners, the people will always need charity. But when they learn how to lead, this all changes.

In fact, this cultural shift is so big that even manufacturing companies are buying in. As one article in a business magazine put it: "The leading companies in the tech industry are reworking their business models to deliver everything-as-service."[30]

This means that future consumers won't just buy a computer. With it they'll buy a lifetime of personalized service from the company that produced it. This model was pioneered by Steve Jobs and other business leaders who saw that service is the future—especially as the millennials and postmillennials grow up and take their leading place in the economy.

Likewise, consumers will no longer just buy a television, a coffee maker, or a car, they'll buy the best service the car company can give—for as long as the owner has it. Elon Musk and Tesla are on the cutting edge of this trend. They want to provide the best service on Earth, and on Mars as well.

> This focus on service is a major positive character trait of the millennial and postmillennial generations.

Literally.

This focus on service is a major positive character trait of the millennial and postmillennial generations, and it is has the potential to effectively solve the problems of not being willing to push outside their comfort zones and having an overblown sense of entitlement.

230

But it is going to take leaders from within these two generations to show the way. That means *you*.

Parents: this means *your* current children, teens, and young adults.

Applying the tools of financial fitness is a great way to start. But don't just think outside the box. Learn to think *inside* the box in order to more creatively think *outside* the box.

That's leadership and innovation.

YOUTH
Call to Action

A. Be sure to do the brainstorming exercise in this chapter. It can greatly help you with your life mission and financial choices.

B. What ways can you imagine combining service and your business goals? Brainstorm a list of possibilities, and write them down.

PARENTS AND OTHER ADULTS
Call to Action

1. Complete Youth Exercise A above. In fact, this exercise may be even more important for adults! Don't skip it. Spend some time and real effort on it. What do you really want? This is a powerful question.

2. Complete Youth Exercise B above. This is very important. Have fun with it, and let your imagination run wild.

"Eureka!"

TOOL #19

"Asset-ize!"

Frequent-Flier Miles...[and other loyalty points have] become a virtual currency of great worth.
—POPULAR SCIENCE

Seventy-five percent of families in the U.S. can't park their cars in the garage because they have too much stuff. It is genuinely a stress builder.
—DEBORAH HEISZ

How to Asset-ize!

Given the quotes above, maybe the focus of this chapter should be how to build businesses renting storage units to people or helping them cash in their various frequent-flyer and other hotel, credit card, and customer loyalty points. Apparently these are only going to increase in demand.

In fact, these are assets. Many of them are dormant assets, but with a little effort they could be turned to useful assets.

Specifically, this chapter is about "asset-izing," and this is a very important (but easily learned) skill. It will, of course, take some effort. But the effort will pay you very positive dividends. Here is how "asset-izing" works. Let's focus on teens first:

- First, you look around at your room and see if there is any of your stuff that you don't really need, want, or like anymore.
- Second, you decide whether to keep it or sell it.
- Third, you run it by your parents to make sure you're not selling your great, great-grandfather's heirloom lapel pin, or anything like it.
- Fourth, you sell it.
- Fifth, you put all of the money into your savings account or into the investment hierarchy we discussed.

You just upgraded your assets. Well done!

Here's a little more help on each of the five steps.

Finding Things

Come on, let's be honest. There's stuff in there you haven't used, or even noticed, for years. Why not turn it into an asset?

Actually, there are a few good reasons to keep some of it. If you received it as a gift from someone in your family, it might hurt their feelings if you sell it. And relationships are one of your most important assets. If you sell the DVD your little sister worked hard to buy for you, you might be losing a more important asset than the amount you get for it.

Just think about it, with each item. Marie Condo's best-selling book *The Life-Changing Magic of Tidying Up* teaches an interesting way to sort through your things.[31] Put everything that you think you might want to sell on the floor (make sure the floor is clear of all your other stuff first!), starting with clothes, then working through your other categories like books, games, etc.[32]

Sorting

When you have all the clothes you might want to sell spread out on the floor, systematically go to each item, touch it, and ask yourself, "Do I still like this? Do I still want this?"[33] If so, put it back in your closet or drawer. If not, put it in the "sell" pile. Repeat this process with everything you might want to sell.

Now, after you've returned the things you don't want to sell to their shelves or other regular spots, put all the things you might sell in a nice, neat pile. Wait a day before selling, so you don't make a mistake.

When the day has passed, look through the pile again and see if there is anything you keep thinking about, or just plain don't want to sell right now. Pull it out and keep it.

The rest of the pile is ready for the next step.

Parent Review

Now tell your parents what you're thinking, and ask them to sort your pile and veto anything they want you to keep. Give them full veto power, and don't argue or lobby. They're your parents, and you need their support in this, so whatever they say goes.

Just smile happily while they go through your things.

Parent Help

When this is done, ask your parents where they think you can get the best price for each item you're going to sell. They may or may not want to spend much time on this, but get as much of their help as they're willing to give.

Take notes while they give you ideas: rummage sale, second-hand store, pawn shop, eBay, a local online buying group, etc.

Thank them for their help, and go research each item on eBay. See if such items have sold in the past and for how much.

Then, if you decide to do a garage sale or go to a secondhand store, you'll know your opportunity cost to sell the item, meaning how much you can likely get on eBay.

Make sure your parents know what you are doing online and approve it.

Put in some real effort, and do your best to sell these items. This is a mini-entrepreneurial project for you. Use it to improve your leadership skills.

Deposit It!

Each time you get paid, put the money in a special envelope in your finances box, and when you're done selling everything, deposit the entire amount into your savings account.

That's "asset-izing."

The Second Mile

Once you have done this, you'll likely want to do it again. But you've given away most of what you have that's for sale. So what can you do?

Since you're now a budding entrepreneur, there are many options. Here are two:

1. Sit down with your parents and tell them about your project and how much money you made. It might only be $25, or it could be a lot more. Tell them you learned a lot and that you've deposited the entire amount into your savings.

Then tell them you have an idea. "What if I did the same thing with the messy garage? Of course, most of that stuff isn't mine, but I promise I'd run every item past you both before I try to sell it. And if you don't want me to sell it, I obviously won't. But if you're okay with me selling it, I'll split the money with you. Or you can choose a percentage that I'd make, if you don't feel that 50/50 is fair.

"I'll be happy with whatever you decide. Oh, and I'll clean the garage up really well in the process. What do you think?"

Some parents will probably like it, and others won't (largely depending on what's in their garage). But if they go for it, you've got another winner. And even at 10% or 20% of what you sell, you'll probably make more than you did on the things from your room. Whatever you make, put it all in your savings account. That's asset-izing.

2. If your parents don't want you to do the garage, or if you do it and you now need yet another asset-izing project, become an asset-izing expert. Tell your brothers and sisters what you did and how much you made, and ask them if they'd like to help you do the same thing for them. But with siblings, only ask for 10% of the income.

And never, ever pressure your siblings to sell something they aren't sure about. In fact, if they're not sure, suggest that they not sell it. They can always sell it later if they decide to. Always have your siblings run items past your parents, just the way you did.

In fact, this usually goes a lot better if you invite your mom or dad to this meeting. Include them in the offer.

"So, Mom, Johnny, Erica, Molly, what do you think? I can start on someone's room or the hall closet or whatever you need today if you want...."

Always be totally honest about the money. Give them their full 90%, and if you need to split a quarter or a dollar to get it right, but can't, split it in their favor—not yours. When you are done with each project and you have your 10%, or even more if your parents hire you, deposit it all in your savings account. Good asset-izing.

Never, ever sell anything without your parents' permission.

It's Your Business

By the way, asset-izing is also a great way to raise a little money when you want to start a business. Just be sure you put the whole amount into your business or your savings. Don't just sell your stuff and buy packs of cards with bubble gum. Or crisp bean burritos with Cherry Sprite.

When you spend the money you get from selling your stuff, you're taking future assets (things you could sell later when you want to start a business or save for a car) and squandering them now. When you asset-ize, put all the money in savings, or invest it in your business.

For Adults

If you are an adult rather than a teen, asset-izing can fulfill the same functions outlined here. It can be a huge blessing, and a big benefit. Sell that old '67 in your garage. Sell your fishing gear that you haven't used for eight years. You get the idea.

But it's very important to follow the rules of asset-izing, no matter your age. Anything that will sell for money is a dormant asset that you already have, so never just sell your dormant assets and then spend the money.

> **It's very important to follow the rules of asset-izing, no matter your age.**

Transfer these dormant assets into cash assets by putting them in your savings account or into business assets by investing in your business.

The Third Rung

Now, all of this brings us to the concept of the third rung. When somebody needs more money, what can he or she do about it? The Temberly family just can't make ends meet. Cody White has been working hard, but he just isn't going to make enough money in time to go on that special senior trip. Carlos Fernandez simply can't pay his bills—when all the income is in, there just isn't enough to cover everything.

Most people respond to this kind of challenge in one of two ways. Rung One: A lot of them start looking for things to cut—no more milk when they buy groceries, cancel the cable TV, start carpooling to work, and so on. Rung Two: The second way people frequently respond to not enough money is by asking for a raise.[34]

To repeat, these are the two predictable rungs of "I need more money fast!":

- Cut expenses
- Try to get a raise

But there is a third rung, or way, to accomplish this. And it very often ends up being the best option. A lot of people don't think about it, but those who make it work frequently find that it helps them a lot more than they expected.

You probably already know what the third rung is. It's finding some way to entrepreneur or otherwise creatively earn a little more money.[35] Words and phrases that describe this kind of extra hustle are numerous, including:

- Become a weekend entrepreneur (using your spare time to start a little business from your home)
- Moonlight (get a second part-time job)
- Find side work (offer yourself online to do things like moving furniture)[36]
- Start a side business (use your evenings to build it)
- Web-preneuring (offering your skills online, like designing websites or keeping someone's accounting books up to date[37])

All of this basically amounts to "asset-izing" your time. And it's surprising how many entrepreneurs trace the story of their business success to just needing some extra cash and trying to do something to help themselves. The third rung is a powerful way to look past the norm, think *outside* and *inside* the box, and improve your life.

> **It's surprising how many entrepreneurs trace the story of their business success to just needing some extra cash and trying to do something to help themselves.**

The options are as numerous as your creativity. When you get outside the box and start doing things to improve your future, a lot of good can happen. Just consider the power of the following words: *"trendsetter...unconventional...disrupter... game-changing...transformational...revolutionize...small changes...do something different right now!"*

Asset-izing can take many forms, but one of the most powerful is when you simply decide that you're going to make some important changes—and create a different future than you imagined. This is asset-izing at its finest.

So don't hold back. Figure out the kind of future you want, and start looking for ways to obtain it! Take action.

(And again, if you are a teen or younger, always run such projects by your parents before you engage them.)

YOUTH
Call to Action

Do you feel an asset-izing project coming on? Make sure your parents know the details and give you permission every step of the way!

PARENTS AND OTHER ADULTS
Call to Action

1. Do you also feel an asset-izing project coming on? Here's the thing: you absolutely must make sure that you run every single item you're thinking about selling past your spouse. Otherwise this can quickly turn into a huge argument.

Also, clearly discuss that you'd like to put all the proceeds into savings before the project even starts.

Give the other person full veto power on whether or not you sell any item. This avoids arguments, and you'll likely still find enough to make the project very worthwhile.

Warning: For some people, their possessions carry a lot of emotional attachments. If you feel resistance, just back off. Or switch the project to only selling things that are your personal items. Even if you do this, it's best to run each item past your spouse. Better safe than sorry.

2. What kind of changes do you need to make in your life in order to get the kind of financial results you really want?

Seriously.

Take some time and think about this.

Write down your ideas.

Make a plan.

Act on it.

(This is the best kind of asset-izing!)

"Get down to brass tacks...."

The Tale of the Lemonade: Practice Being an Entrepreneur

Raise hungry kids.
—TERRI BRADY

What would you dream if you knew you couldn't fail?
It takes just as much effort to pursue
a small dream as big dream.
—ORRIN WOODWARD

Christine's Venture

Christine decided she wanted to run a lemonade stand and make a little extra cash. The neighborhood was holding a big rummage sale, and this seemed like the perfect opportunity. Her little brother wanted to be part of it, and on the day of the sale they made the arrangements, mixed the lemonade, put up the stand, hung signs, and began selling. It went well for a quite a while, but then she noticed that sales suddenly dropped off rather sharply. She wondered what could have caused the change.

With a little investigation, she found that a neighbor boy had opened up a competing lemonade stand around the corner. Now, when people wanted that second cup of ice-cold lemonade, they didn't have to walk all the way back to her stand. They could just go to the competition.

Christine had a choice to make. She could either settle for lower sales or figure out some way to get things going again. She decided to rally, by adding coffee, muffins, and other options to her menu.

Word got around, and her sales quickly picked up again.

> These kinds of entrepreneurial ventures help young people get a head start on their financial life. They learn important lessons as they deal with the issues that invariably come up, and with the help of attentive parent mentoring, they can learn even more.

But then Christine had to deal with a partnership challenge. Her brother got tired and wanted to quit. Later, now rested, he wanted to buy back in. She negotiated the details with him while continuing to sell.

All in all, it was a very good day. In fact, she was so enthused that she later repeated the project and sold lemonade and other items to raise money for an orphanage.

These kinds of entrepreneurial ventures help young people get a head start on their financial life. They learn important lessons as they deal with the issues that invariably come up, and with the help of attentive parent mentoring, they can learn even more.

Jake's New Gig First paragraph should have normal indents, same as body text.

For example, in Jake's new town he couldn't go door-to-door and pitch people work projects for their yard or farm. But he still wanted to make some money one summer, so he went around looking for possible jobs. McDonald's had some openings, but he didn't like the idea of being inside so much of the day. The city pool needed a few more lifeguards, but he'd have to take a training class first, and he'd miss the first month of getting paid.

When he spoke with his mother, he lamented the fact that in the city he couldn't do the kinds of jobs he had back in their rural community. His mom recommended that he find out what really worked in this town—not pine away after the old one.

He asked around, and drove through town with his dad, and they both noticed that there were a lot of snow cone shacks, little soda shops, and other small outlets for summer drinks. Some of them had nothing more than a shade tent, a snow-cone machine, and a few chairs. The town received a lot of summer tourists, and these kinds of little venues were obviously popular.

Jake loved working with people, and he quickly fell in love with the idea of spending the summer selling ice cream, snow cones, and soda drinks to tourists. His dad helped him build a little sales shack, and they found a business in town that rented them a sales spot for just $100 a month.

A city representative came by and sold them a seasonal sales license, and they were in business. Jake looked into buying a snow cone machine but decided to take a less expensive route by purchasing soda and ice cream bars and keeping them in two big ice coolers.

He sold well through June, and by the Fourth of July he had hired his brother to work with him. The demand increased through July and into early August. Jake had already learned in June that on Mondays and Tuesdays he didn't sell very much—but on Thursdays, Fridays, and Saturdays he sold a lot. There were always more tourists on the weekends.

They decided to take Mondays and Tuesdays off. Sometimes they sold on Wednesdays, if they were in the mood. Other Wednesdays they just enjoyed the summer. But Jake found that when they did open shop on Wednesday, they did better on Thursday—probably because they had everything in place and ready to go early Thursday morning.

By the end of the summer they had grossed over $4,200 and spent $797.20 on materials. Jake paid his brother $5 an hour plus two free ice creams or sodas a day, and this cost him just over $960. (His brother purchased over $80 in treats back from him over the summer!) He also paid $110 for company T-shirts that he and his brother wore at work, and $300 for rent.

Jake ended up netting over $2000, and he had a lot of free time to enjoy the summer. He also met a lot of new people and had a lot of fun.

> There are many similar stories, and they show us how many ways there are for young people to practice being entrepreneurial, make some extra cash, and learn important lessons for the future.

Multiple Lessons

There are many similar stories, and they show us how many ways there are for young people to practice being entrepreneurial, make some extra cash, and learn important lessons for the future. The skills of leadership, focus, follow-through, and other important lessons that come from such ventures are almost impossible to replicate in any other way.

One common theme in such experiences is that parental support and guidance usually make the difference between struggling projects and those that really succeed. Another is that parents can make a huge positive contribution by frequently discussing with the young person what lessons he or she is learning.

Imagine just how much Christine and Jake, and others like them, would learn if they also applied all the tools of financial fitness. They'd save a great deal of money, they'd give some of what they've earned to help others, they'd keep their receipts and record them on their income statements, they'd learn to study and understand their financial numbers, and they'd become better at negotiating, pleasing the customer, working through various issues with their employees, estimating how much inventory they'd need on hand and making adjustments, marketing, etc.

They would also learn a lot about the value of money, wise spending, budgeting, building assets, thinking outside (and inside) the box, initiative, hard work, and leadership. All of these skills are invaluable. And nothing teaches them nearly as well as actual, real-life experience.

Even More!

In fact, teen entrepreneurial projects naturally teach many of the tools of wise money and financial fitness. As young people like Christine and Jake conceive of, plan, and implement such projects, and deal with the inevitable little challenges that arise during the journey, they are taught the following key lessons:

My life has an important purpose.
I may not be sure yet what it is, but I know I have one,
and I want to prepare for it as well as I can while I'm young.

I need to be a good leader.

I'm not dependent on my allowance to make money.
I can do other things as well.

I am responsible to earn money
for the things I need and want.

Making money takes real work,
and I'm going to save a lot of what I make.

I'm also going to give part of what I earn
to help people who are in need.
I want to improve the world.

I won't waste my money.
It took too much hard work to earn it.
I'm going to save it for what I really want.

I don't need anyone to give me the money I need.
I can go and find ways to earn it!

Entrepreneurial ventures usually
earn me more money than jobs or assignments.

I want to build assets.

I need to keep my receipts and other important documents.

I need to record income and expenses
and study these numbers to really know what I'm doing.

A preplanned budget actually
gives me huge power over my money!

I'm building my savings.
It's so exciting to watch it grow!

Each method of handling money
(cash, debit cards, checks, credit cards)
has important details that I need to understand and use wisely.
I can't just wing it!

Honesty and integrity are the only way!

As the leader, I am responsible.
If something needs fixing, I need to make sure it gets fixed.
If something needs to be improved, I need to make sure
it gets improved.

The Leadership Class in Your Neighborhood

Again, such lessons are price-less. If a local school or community college offered a class to teach young people these lessons—and

If you want your teens to really become financially fit and master the tools of smart money, get them involved in practicing entrepreneurial projects.

guaranteed a high rate of success—most parents would flock to enroll their teens.

Guess what? Small, manageable, entrepreneurial ventures often do this incredibly well. Time after time. Success after success. Teen after teen.

Yet only a few families help their teens engage in such projects.

Again, this kind of success requires a bit of parental support and some parent time spent really talking about the lessons each teen is learning. But the results are significant, and lasting.

If you want your teens to really become financially fit and master the tools of smart money, get them involved in practicing entrepreneurial projects. The lessons of the lemonade stand are priceless. They'll pay real (literally, real) dividends in the years to come.

For Adults

By the way, these same principles apply to adults as well. If you want to get on the business-owner track but just haven't been able to make the leap—for whatever reason—try practicing mini-entrepreneurial projects. Focus on areas you are passionate about, and don't invest very much money to begin with. Take small steps and many iterations, getting better with each.

Then adjust and repeat. It won't take long for you to find enjoyment and maybe even increased life direction from entrepreneurial practice projects.

YOUTH
Call to Action

A. Brainstorm a list of possible entrepreneurial projects you could do. Write them down.

B. Discuss the list with your parents, and talk about turning one of them into a reality. Discuss timing, costs, and details. Listen to your parents' recommendations, ideas, and warnings. Really think about this project.

C. Implement an entrepreneurial project.

D. Discuss what you learned with your parents. What would you do better if you could do it all again?

PARENTS AND OTHER ADULTS
Call to Action

Seriously consider implementing a mini-entrepreneurial project yourself.

"Take the bull by the horns...."

CONCLUSION

Your Finances
Twenty Years from Now

Many people appear to be tiptoeing through life
trying to get to death safely.
—CHRIS BRADY

It's True!

Twenty years from now, you will either be living the life of your dreams...or not. If you are, a few things will be true. First, you'll be applying most or all of the money tools outlined in this book. Second, you'll have assets because you will have spent time effectively building assets. Third, you'll have a clear life purpose (one that includes important service in the world), and you'll be focused on making it happen.

This is true.

If you're not living the life of your dreams twenty years from now, these things probably won't be true. They certainly aren't true for most of the 80 percent of people who don't like their jobs and are frustrated in some (or many) ways with their lives.

The good news is that you largely get to choose your future. You get to choose whether you'll do the things that bring happiness, success, and fulfillment. You get to choose whether you'll use these tools to become truly financially fit. You get to choose whether you'll help other people do the same.

All of these choices will have a huge influence on where you are—and *who* you are—twenty years from now.

Your choices will determine your future.

By the way, this is true whether you are 13 years old, age 63, or some other age. You get to choose, and your choices will determine your future.

Dream a Little

For example, what do you really want most out of life? If you could change one thing about your life right now, what would it be?

These are profound questions. And in most cases, whatever your answers, you have the power to choose them.

It might take some time. And it will almost certainly require some hard work. But you get to choose. Twenty years from today, you'll have the life you choose—starting right now.

It's okay to use your imagination more. Do you want to spend more time with your family? Make a plan and get started. Do you want to buy a bigger house with a large yard? Make a plan and get started. Do you want to sit in the best seats at your favorite opera or professional sporting event? Make a plan and get started.

Whatever you want, you can have it. Make a plan, get the right mentors, and get started.

Do you want to engage in "voluntourism" helping people in Africa? Make a plan and get started. Do you want to travel the hemisphere on your own yacht, visiting all the little towns and cities along the way? Make a plan and get started.

Whatever you want, you can have it. Make a plan, get the right mentors, and get started.

Tool #4 is applicable here: Go and Find!

If you want your dream life, you've got to go and find it. But don't wait twenty years and just hope it shows up one day. It won't. Go after it, starting now.

And start by dreaming. What do you want? What do you want in your life? What do you want your life to be like in twenty years?

Close your eyes and picture it.

The Thing Is…

The truth is, you can have it. But you're going to have to go and get it. That's how life works. Now, of course, it doesn't always turn out exactly as you planned. Life has a habit of giving us twists and turns along the way. But you can have what you want in this life, twists and all.

You just have to know what it is and do the things that will bring it. The tools in this book are some of those things. If you don't apply them, you probably won't have a lot of what you want twenty years from now.

That's blunt. But it's true.

These tools are that powerful. And they work.

In fact, let's boil them down to their most basic format. This is different than the table of contents. This is the real list of the top tools you'll need, turned into principles.

Take the time to read each of these principles. They are very important, and they can greatly help you have the life you really, truly want:

Tool #1: Take Responsibility for Your Own Financial Fitness

Tool #2: Always Save and Give *Before* You Spend

Tool #3: Practice Delayed Gratification and Wise Spending

Tool #4: Don't Wait for the Life or Finances You Want, Go and Find What You Want!

Tool #5: However You Make a Living, Make Part (or All) of Your Work Entrepreneurial

Tool #6: Build Assets, and Keep Building Assets

Tool #7: Keep Good Financial Records

Tool #8: Carefully Watch Your Own Personal and Business Financial Numbers

Tool #9: Follow a Wise Savings-Oriented Budget

Tool #10: Save Cash, and Also Save in Bank Accounts

Tool #11: Wisely Use Checking Accounts and Debit Cards

Tool #12: Follow the 5 Rules of Credit Cards, or Don't Use Them

Tool #13: Always Know the Hidden Costs Before You Buy

Tool #14: Tap Into a Lot of Owner Benefits

Tool #15: Wisely Use Insurance as an Asset

Tool #16: Don't Invest in Anything You Don't Deeply Understand

Tool #17: Invest in Levels 1–5, and Carefully in 6

Tool #18: Think Outside the Box by Focusing *Inside* the Box

Tool #19: Learn to Turn Dormant Assets into Productive Ones

Tool #20: Practice Being Entrepreneurial (and You Eventually Will Be!)

Remember...

The choice is yours. As Chris Brady put it: "Twenty years from now, what will you wish you had done today?"

Make no mistake: That day twenty years from now *will* come.

The question is, will you be where you want to be when it does? The answer depends on you, and it will largely depend on how well you apply these 20 vital tools of true financial fitness.

If you want to move on in life,
replace bad habits that hold you back
with better ones that propel you forward....
—ORRIN WOODWARD

FINANCIAL GLOSSARY

Accounting: The process of keeping track of personal and business financial transactions.

Affluent: Prosperous.

Annuity: Money paid to you each year, or on another regular interval, based on a previously agreed-upon arrangement. Usually involves you paying in a lot of money to the fund first.

Appraisal: Analysis of a property to determine its market value.

Appreciation: The increase of an asset's value over time. (Contrast: Depreciation, which is the opposite.)

Asset: Something that brings you cash over time or that can be turned into cash. (Contrast: Liability, which is the opposite.)

Asset-ize: To turn dormant assets into actual assets. See details in Tool #19.

Asset Path, The: The choice to use your work life building assets, rather than building mostly expenses and/or debts.

B&P Record: Separating your personal from your business expenses, and recording your business expenses on a ledger or spreadsheet.

Balance Sheet: Listing of all a person's or business's assets and liabilities.

Bank Run: When many depositors rush to a bank to withdraw their funds immediately because they think the bank is going to fail.

Barter: The trade or exchange of goods or services without the use of currency, e.g. trading an apple for an orange. (Compare: Currency)

Bear Market: A stock market with decreasing prices or values. (Compare: Bull Market, which is the opposite)

Bond: A security you can purchase from a business or government entity which pays a set rate of interest to you over time—and can only be redeemed at certain predetermined times.

Boomers: The generation born between the late 1940s and the mid 1960s.

Brady System, The: A system of allowances for children and youth that trains leaders and financially fit young people. See details in Tool #1.

Brady System, The Second: A system of teaching young people financial leadership and responsibility by encouraging them to make entrepreneurial proposals instead of just seeking payment for chores. Described in detail in Tool #4.

Broker: An intermediary in a financial exchange, usually paid a commission for services rendered or even a percentage of the size of the transaction.

Budget: A planning tool whereby individuals, families, or organizations preplan their income and expenditures.

Bull Market: A stock market with increasing prices or values. (Contrast: Bear Market, which is the opposite)

Business Cycle: The ups and downs of an economy.

Capital: Money that is used to pay for goods or services that are intended to increase the income of a business or individual. For example: the money used to buy a building from which to sell your company's goods to the public.

Capital Gain: The profit from selling an asset. For example, you buy a house for $150,000 and later sell it for $175,000. Your capital gain is $25,000.

CDs (Certificates of Deposit): A type of savings that pays you interest for a period of time, and you must wait until the predetermined time to collect your interest and/or get your principal back. A bond issued by a bank.

Chainsaw Principle, The: Some tools—like chainsaws, firearms, vehicles, and credit cards—shouldn't be used unless you know the rules and always follow them with precision.

Collateral: An asset you give to a creditor to hold in order to "secure" a loan. When you pay back the loan, the creditor returns the asset or the claim to the asset.

Commerce: Business activity. Trade.

Commodity: A common product used in general consumption on a massive scale. For example: wheat, steel, cars, socks, gold, etc.

Compound Interest: A loan arrangement where interest is paid or charged on both the principal amount of the loan and also the interest that's already been charged.

Consumer: A person who buys a product.

Contract: A written agreement between two or more people or organizations.

Credit: Obtaining money, goods, or services based on the promise that you'll pay for them later.

Creditor: A person or organization to whom you owe a debt. (Contrast: Debtor, which is the opposite)

Currency: Money used to purchase things. (Contrast: Barter)

Debt: Any money, goods, or services you owe to a person or organization.

Debtor: A person who owes a debt. (Contrast: Creditor, which is the opposite)

Deficit: The amount of money spent beyond what was planned for in the budget.

Demand (See: Law of Supply and Demand)

Deposit: The amount you put into your bank account. (Contrast: Withdrawal, which is the opposite)

Depreciation: The amount an asset decreases in value over time. For example, your car is likely worth less today than it was two years ago when you bought it. (Contrast: Appreciation, which is the opposite)

Depression: A period where the economy experiences a major decrease in growth, commercial activity, and employment.

Delayed Gratification: Not buying now so that you'll have better options later. (Contrast: Instant Gratification, which is the opposite)

Dividend: A payment you receive for a stock you own; it comes from the annual profits of the company that issued the stock.

Division of Labor: Dividing a project up into many parts. For example, in most factories one or a few people do a certain job, while others do other tasks. Together these tasks build whatever the factory is producing.

Down Payment: Money you pay at the beginning of a loan, along with the promise to pay the rest of the loan later.

Duty: A tax put on a product by a government, usually on imports.

Entitlement: A sense that somebody owes you something, even when they don't.

Entrepreneur: A person who starts a business. Entrepreneurs usually reap many of the rewards of the organization's success but also bear the risks.

Expenditure: The amount you spend on a good or service. An expense. (Contrast: Income)

Export: A good or service sold in another country. (Contrast: Import)

Fiat Money: Currency printed by the government, not exchangeable for gold or silver. Causes inflation, and hurts the business cycle. Governments use fiat money to increase their own buying power, at the expense of the people.

Free Enterprise: An economic arrangement where everyone is treated equally before the law with a minimum of government regulation, and in which businesses are allowed to start and operate freely on their own.

Glut: Where there are too many of any certain product or service in the market.

Gold Standard: Where the currency is gold and silver, requiring governments to avoid debt or the printing of money and to spend only what they are able to take in through taxes.

Gross: The amount of income you have before you deduct expenses. (Contrast: Net)

Identify Theft: When a hacker or other person steals your social security number, bank account numbers, or other personal information and uses it to access your finances, spend your money, or otherwise try to profit from your private information.

Import: A product that came from another nation. (Contrast: Export, which is the opposite)

Income: The money you bring in. (Contrast: Expenditure, which is the opposite)

Inflation: A decrease in the value of the currency and its buying power.

Instant Gratification: Wanting what you want right now. Often leads to poor financial decisions, including debt. (Contrast: Delayed Gratification, which is the opposite)

Insurance: Protection you buy to shield you from catastrophe.

Investment: Buying an asset with the expectation that its value will increase.

Laissez-faire: From the French language, meaning "hands off the people," or "let the people choose." This phrase communicates that government should leave people free to do as they decide, as long as they don't hurt anyone else.

Law of Diminishing Returns: With the use of each additional unit, the value of each unit declines. For example, if you sit down and begin eating hamburgers, the first one will give you more value than the fourteenth burger.

Law of Supply and Demand: As the demand for a product or service increases, the price rises. (Of course, many other factors can influence the price.)

Layoff: When a company cuts back its production and removes workers from their jobs.

Ledger: A chart used to record and tally financial numbers.

Level 1 Investing: Invest in yourself, your knowledge, experience, and your primary business (a business you own).

Level 2 Investing: Invest in an emergency fund. Also called a rainy-day fund. Save at least $1,000 in this fund, and then build it up to at least $5,000. Aim for at least 3-4 months of expenses.

Level 3 Investing: Invest in sensible survival prep, such as food storage, silver coins, cash, batteries, etc.

Level 4 Investing: Savings. Build your savings, and keep building it. Most people should put all their investments into Levels 1–4 and minimize any investments in Levels 5–7.

Level 5 Investing: Once you have a lot of money in savings, you can sometimes get a better return on some of it by putting it into CDs, bonds, or your own business. Only use some of your savings this way, and carefully research the details beforehand.

Level 6 Investing: Some people make money investing in stocks and real estate. A lot of people don't. In fact, many people lose money in these ventures. The rule of thumb is to avoid Level 6 Investments, unless your primary business is stocks or real estate and you truly know what you are doing.

Level 7 Investing: Once you have some assets, a lot of people will probably want to invest your money. Don't invest in anything unless you really know the business, the field, the details, the people, and what will and won't work. Only invest in what you really know and deeply understand.

Liability: A debt. What you owe. (Contrast: Asset, which is the opposite)

Macroeconomics: The part of economics that deals with the whole nation/economy. (Compare: Microeconomics)

Market Economy: An economy where most of the owners are private, rather than government. (See: Free Enterprise, Socialist Economy, Mixed Economy)

Microeconomics: The part of economics that deals with individuals, businesses, and products, etc. (Compare: Macroeconomics)

Millennials: The generation born between the early 1980s and the early 2000s. (See: Postmillennials)

Mixed Economy: An economy that contains elements of both a market economy and a socialist economy. Nearly always becomes increasingly socialistic over time. (See: Market Economy, Free Enterprise, Socialist Economy)

Monetary Policy: A government's use of printing/issuing currency to supposedly regulate the economy. (See: Gold Standard)

Mortgage: The loan agreement between lenders and buyers of a home or property.

Mutual Fund: A company whose focus is investments. When people invest in mutual funds, they own partial shares of numerous stocks or other securities.

National Debt: The debt of the national government.

Net: The amount that remains when you add up all income and deduct all expenditures. (Compare: Gross)

Opportunity Cost: In any given choice or transaction, what you would lose out on being able to do by instead choosing a different option.

Overdraft: When you write a check or checks for more money than you have in your account.

PDCA: Plan, do, check, adjust. The ongoing process of planning, taking action to implement the plan, checking to see what is working and what isn't, and adjusting accordingly.

Permanent Life Insurance: Provides a death benefit plus the cash value you build up as you pay for your life insurance over the years, allowing you to invest money that will go to your loved ones after your death. Whole life insurance is also a great way to grow your wealth tax free, because it has a "cash value" component that builds up over the years that you can always borrow from. (Compare: Term Life Insurance)

Personal Property: The things owned by a person or organization that are not land or buildings. For example: furniture, clothes, etc. (Contrast: Real Property)

Postmillennials: The generation born in the early 2000s and since.

Private Sector: The part of the economy not controlled by government. (Contrast: Public Sector)

Public Sector: The part of the economy controlled by the government. (Contrast: Private Sector)

REIT (Real Estate Investment Trust): An investment where you own partial shares in a number of pieces of real estate.

Real Property: The land or buildings owned by a person or organization. (Contrast: Personal Property)

Recession: When the economy isn't growing, or is consistently decreasing.

Reconcile Your Checkbook: Comparing your monthly bank statement (from your checking account) with your personal ledger of checking account activity, to ensure that your numbers are accurate.

Regulation: Laws a government uses to control business and other private entities.

Savings: The first thing you pay when you earn or receive any money. An asset.

Securities: The papers proving that you own stocks, bonds, etc.; also, another term for those tradable items themselves.

Services: Work done for others in exchange for compensation.

Socialist Economy: An economy where most of the ownership is governmental rather than private. (See: Market Economy, Free Enterprise, Mixed Economy)

Spreadsheet: An electronic ledger that records and tallies financial numbers. Many financial software programs include various kinds of spreadsheets (some use the term spreadsheet, while some do not).

Standard of Living: The products and services the average family typically enjoys in a given nation, place, or generation.

Stock: A share of ownership in a corporation.

Stock Exchange: The place where stocks, bonds, and securities are bought and sold. Also called a stock market.

Supply (See: Law of Supply and Demand)

Tariff: A government tax on an import.

10,000 Hour Mastery: Putting in enough time and gaining enough experience in your primary work that you really understand it in depth and in detail. (See: Invest in What You Know)

Term Life Insurance: Gives financial help to your family or whomever you designate as the recipient of your life insurance money if you die (called a *death benefit*). Term life insurance coverage is relatively inexpensive, but it times out when you get old. (Compare: Permanent Life Insurance)

Third Rung, The: When people can't pay all their bills, the First Rung is to begin cutting expenses, the Second Rung is to ask for a raise, and the Third Rung is creatively find ways to bring in more money through entrepreneurial and/or other innovations.

Trade: Economic or business activity. Commerce.

Withdrawal: The amount you take out of your bank account. (Compare: Deposit, which is the opposite)

Xers: The generation born between the late 1960s and the early 1980s. Also known as Gen X or Generation X.

NOTES

(Endnotes)

1   "Talking Shop: The Buzz," *Marie Claire*, January 2016, p. 37.

2   Ibid.

3   Ibid.

4   Ibid.

5   See, for example, Michael Gerber, The E-Myth Revisited.

6   Investopedia website, "Banking: Safeguarding Your Accounts."

7   Ibid, "Debit Cards."

8   "Choose the Best Bank for You," *Consumer Reports*, January 2016, p. 31.

9   Ibid.

10   Ibid.

11   Ibid.

12   Paul Leicester Ford, 1898, *The Honorable Peter Stirling*, New York: Henry Holt and Company, p. 12.

13   *Financial Fitness*, p. 152.

14   See *The Warren Buffett Way*.

15   LouAnn Loften, "Invest Like a Girl (And Warren Buffett)," *U.S. News and World Report*, Special Edition: Special Report: *Secrets of the Rich*, 2012.

16   *Financial Fitness*, p. 148.

17   See example in Dana Hudepohl, "Satisfying her heart's desire," *More*, November 2015.

18   Ibid.

19   Ibid.

20   *Financial Fitness*, p. 152.

21   Stephen Palmer, *Manifest Destiny: Choosing a Life of Greatness*, (paperback edition), p. 146.

22   Ibid.

23   Ibid.

24   See Matthew Hutson, "Beyond Happiness: The Upside of Feeling Down," *Psychology Today*, January/February 2015, p. 53.

25   Ibid.

26   For more on the millennial generation, see: Neil Howe and William Strauss, *The Fourth Turning*; Neil Howe and William Strauss, *Millennials Rising*; Mitchell Augustine, *Millennials: The Connected Generation*; Chip Espinoza and Mick Ukleja, *Managing the Millennials*; Thomas S. Rainer and Jess Rainer, *The Millennials*.

27   Ibid.

28   Ibid.

29   See, for example, Melissa Biggs Bradley, "The rewards of volun-tourism," *More*, December 2015/January 2016.

30   *strategy + business*, Winter 2014, p. 2.

31   See Hollie Deese, "The Tidy Home Tome," *USA Today: Modern Woman*, Fall/Winter 2015.

32   Ibid.

33   See ibid.

34   See, for example, Farnoosh Torabi, "Don't always focus on a raise," *USA Today: Modern Woman*, Fall/Winter 2015.

35   Ibid.

36   Ibid.

37   Meryl Davids Landau, with Rett Fisher, "8 Creative Ways to Boost Your Income," *U.S. News and World Report,* Special Edition: Special Report: *Secrets of the Rich,* 2012.

FINANCIAL FITNESS PROGRAM

Get Out of Debt and Stay Out of Debt!

FREE PERSONAL WEBSITE

SIGN UP AND TAKE ADVANTAGE OF THESE FREE FEATURES:

- Personal website
- Take your custom assessment test
- Build your own profile
- Share milestones and successes with partners and friends
- Post videos and photos
- Receive daily info "nuggets"

FINANCIAL FITNESS BASIC PROGRAM

The first program to teach all three aspects of personal finance: defense, offense, and playing field. Learn the simple, easy-to-apply principles that can help you shore up your resources, get out of debt, and build stability for a more secure future. It's all here, including a comprehensive book, companion workbook, and 8 audios that amplify the teachings from the books.

Also available DIGITALLY!

financialfitnessinfo.com

FINANCIAL FITNESS MASTER CLASS

Buy it once and use it forever! Designed to provide a continual follow-up to the principles learned in the Basic Program, this ongoing educational support offers over 6 hours of video and over 14 hours of audio instruction that walk you through the workbook, step by step. Perfect for individual or group study.
6 videos, 15 audios

FINANCIAL FITNESS TRACK AND SAVE

The Financial Fitness Program teaches you how to get out of debt, build additional streams of income, and properly take advantage of tax deductions. Now, with this subscription, we give you the tools to do so. The Tracker offers mobile expense tracking tools and budgeting software, while the Saver offers you thousands of coupons and discounts to help you save money every day.

THE WEALTH HABITS SERIES

The Wealth Habits series is designed to help you prosper through consistent, ongoing, simple, and enjoyable financial literacy education. You will learn timeless principles about how to better handle your money, and timely commentary on the current economic forces affecting the "playing

field" upon which we all must participate. Small doses of information applied consistently over time can produce enormous results through the formation of new and profitable habits. This is what the Wealth Habits series is all about.

The Wealth Habits series will put you in a unique position. You will know something that only a few people in the world know. You will know the principles of financial fitness. You have the power to not only develop financial fitness but also to positively impact the lives of those around you. And the time to act is NOW.

LEARN TO NOT ONLY *SURVIVE*, BUT *THRIVE* DURING TOUGH ECONOMIC TIMES!